SERIAL GIRLS

SERIAL GIRLS
FROM BARBIE TO PUSSY RIOT

MARTINE DELVAUX

Translated by Susanne de Lotbinière-Harwood

Between the Lines
Toronto

Serial Girls: From Barbie to Pussy Riot

Originally published in French as *Les filles en série: Des Barbies aux Pussy Riot,*
© 2013 Les Éditions du remue-ménage, Montreal www.editions-rm.ca
English translation © 2016 Susanne de Lotbinière-Harwood

First published in English translation in 2016 by
Between the Lines
401 Richmond St. W., Studio 277
Toronto, Ontario M5V 3A8 Canada
1-800-718-7201   www.btlbooks.com

Certain passages of this book were first published in French in the publications *Liberté*, *À bâbord*, *Tangence*, *Frontières*, and *Globe*.

Library and Archives Canada Cataloguing in Publication

Delvaux, Martine, 1968
[Filles en série. English]
        Serial girls : from Barbie to Pussy Riot / Martine Delvaux; translator, Susanne de Lotbinière-Harwood.
Translation of: Les filles en série, des Barbies aux Pussy Riot.
Issued in print and electronic formats.
ISBN 978-1-77113-185-8 (paperback). – ISBN 978-1-77113-186-5 (epub).
ISBN 978-1-77113-187-2 (pdf)

1. Women – Social conditions. 2. Women in literature. 3. Women in motion pictures.
4. Girls in popular culture. I. Lotbinière-Harwood, Susanne de, translator II. Title.
III. Title: Filles en série. English
HQ1150.D3413 2016   305.42   C2016-904716-4
                                                                             C2016-904717-2

Cover design by Jennifer Tiberio
Page preparation by Steve Izma
Printed in Canada

We acknowledge for their financial support of our publishing activities the Government of Canada through the Canada Book Fund, the Canada Council for the Arts, which last year invested $153 million to bring the arts to Canadians throughout this country, and the Government of Ontario through the Ontario Arts Council, the Ontario Book Publishers Tax Credit program, and the Ontario Media Development Corporation.

We acknowledge the financial support of the Government of Canada through the National Translation Program for Book Publishing, an initiative of the *Roadmap for Canada's Official Languages 2013–2018: Education, Immigration, Communities*, for our translation activities.

Contents

Acknowledgements

Thank you to Amanda Crocker and Dave Molenhuis for their amazing work on this book! Thanks to Patrick Harrop for constant support, to Valérie Lebrun for her help throughout the final stages of this process, and to Eléonore Delvaux-Beaudoin for working with me on the pictures!

Barbie Head Bracelet from WordPress blog https://diynotuiuc.wordpress.com

Introduction

I Is a Girl

It was the summer of 2012. Every evening we would go out, improvising new routes through the city under the watch of police clad in black, in helmets, batons in hand. We lived for leaflets, articles, op-eds, TV news bulletins, meetings, and demonstrations. Nothing else existed apart from what was being described as a revolution. The student cause had driven part of Quebec's population out onto the streets. Social networks were taken over. The noise of the *casserole* rose like the sounds of shared rage.

I too was out on the street. Some evenings I joined in and banged on my saucepan on the balcony with my daughter. Other nights I went onto the streets to march, fading into the crowd. I mingled with the girls marching and chanting slogans. We moved forward side by side, in step with each other. And in the street the boys were always there too. Fathers, sons, colleagues, friends, militants . . . brothers in arms. They were everywhere amid the anonymous crowd, everywhere, like us. Girls. I would ask myself what it all meant – girls assembled, brought together by a cause. Feminist strikers were approaching the strike differently, often struggling in different ways and for different reasons. The spectacle of their bodies in collectivity undoubtedly spoke of other things.

I could hear Virginia Woolf, in her *Three Guineas*, standing up to men who wanted to speak *in the name of women*. She cried: "Not in our name!" That is, we experienced the world differently, and even within the context of a struggle, one that concerned everybody, women had to demand to be heard. I turned my attention to the events and observed that the mobilized female students, these militant feminist strikers, were proof of a particular kind of engagement, one where their position in the anonymity of the struggle remained singular. Though Michel Foucault has clearly shown the power of resistance that resides in the production of the common good as opposed to the private interiority and assigned identities, the fact remains that for the feminist strikers, anonymity needed to be experienced differently. For, in order to prevent this becoming-revolutionary from being used as an alibi for domination and domestication, it had to go hand in hand with good use of the singular: it is necessary, always and everywhere, to keep thinking the feminine.

Through these feminist strikers, I thought I saw Woolf's imagined Outsiders' Society rising up. Alongside their peers, companions in the struggle and co-demonstrators, they occupied the margin, an intermediary position between collective commitment and that place of perpetual foreignness, which is the feminist's lot in society. Shit-disturbers, party-poopers, they are neither nice little girls nor anonymous strikers. Instead, they embody the Ungovernable, which is, writes Giorgio Agamben, "both the point of origin and vanishing point of all politics."[1]

It is this Ungovernable that interests me, and within it I find *serial girls*.

o o o

Serial girls are a series of girls who look alike, whose movements are perfectly aligned, evolving side by side in harmony, indistinguishable one from the other except in clothing detail, like a pair of shoes, or hair colour or skin tone or slightly differing curves. . . . Machine-girls, photo-girls, showgirls, shop-girls, trophy-girls . . . they present the illusion of perfection. I could see these girls everywhere. They seemed to form both a ballet troupe and an army corps. They were cannon-fodder girls, manufactured by the factory of everyday misogyny, but they resisted their commodification. They were girls rising up from the dead.

Playing with Barbies, going to a Rockettes show, or consuming images of naked women in porn magazines . . . they're all something bordering on necrophilia. They all amount to consuming an object that does not react, that does not respond, and that anaesthetizes us through the device of repetition. In our so-called enlightened society, serial girls are candy that feeds a most trivial craving: comfort and intellectual laziness. They respond to a fascistic, perverse, and pleasurable desire for sameness.

This sameness is white and thin. It bears a standard of sizable breasts, a small waist, a flat stomach, shapely long legs, and long straight blond hair. This Western standard is given as universal form, to which all women around the globe (whoever they are, whatever the colour of their skin, whether they are cis or trans) end up being compared to. This is the "ideal" that I am interested in uncovering here: an image that is oblivious to its true colours, its own politics; a hegemonic image that gives itself as universal, cancelling out the place of real women (in particular women of colour and non-cis women), and erasing (effectively or symbolically) actual human beings, their materiality, their specificity, and their differences.

So this is why, when faced with the Tiller Girls, the Busby Berkeley dancers, the Crazy Horse girls, the Spice Girls, while watching models strutting the catwalks, looking at teams of gymnasts or of synchronized swimmers . . . this is why, when faced with *serial girls*, I ask: Who are the *serial killers*?[2] Along with Walter Benjamin, I wonder if, through the mechanical reproduction of girls, we are trying to kill off their aura with impunity, and how girls, the girls, will manage to survive.

What is the point of this generic "becoming" of women that occurs by way of the series? What does the series mean in terms of *gender*? What is the ultimate meaning of this idealization of a perfectly proportioned female body, an element that, as seen in the world of architecture, is foundational and destined to be repeated? What is the difference between seriality put forward in the name of power (think, for example, of the army, of the representatives of law and order) and the objectification of women that operates through relations relying on seriality? These are two radically opposite ways of engendering a gendered being. There is a great disparity between a series of F-18 pilots executing spectacular aerial manoeuvres to produce an image of power and the image of excessively thin girls parading in excessively tight clothes, or all lifting their legs in unison in a demanding gymnastics display done purely for aesthetic purposes . . . and every example of this difference merely widens the gap.

I wanted to write this book in a way similar to the series that fascinate me: as a sequence of images, of figures that always show slight differences. A book that unfolds like a series, in order to conjure up the figure of serial girls and explore its power of resistance: how it plays, how it breaks out of itself. And so this book develops like an extended metaphor; it makes visible the figures, images, and stories that bring serial girls to life. My gaze seeks out and recognizes all these girls as I connect them to each other, placing them side by side in an assembly-line formation.

I am like these girls.

I, too, am part of the series.

The Caryatid Porch of the Erechtheion, Athens, 1865, Dimitrios Constantin, photographer

1

Serial Girls

"It's a girl!" cries the doctor upon seeing the newborn – a performative act sealing her identity. Welcome to this world! From now on, you will be a girl.

It's a Girl is the title of Evan Grae Davis's 2011 documentary about femicide, the quasi-systematic elimination of girls. Millions of girls mistreated, neglected, kidnapped, raped, murdered . . . killed or left to die. According to the U.N., two hundred million girls are missing throughout the world today.[1] A silent war against girls.

One day, while reading a magazine article, I come upon a dialogue between a mother and her daughter. The girl asks, "Mom, what is a girl?" The mother answers, "A girl is somebody who won't remain one for very long." I came upon this dialogue when my daughter was five years old, and one evening, as my hand reached to turn off her bedroom light, well tucked into her little bed, she asked, "Mom, is it true that some people hurt children?" My daughter is ten now. She is becoming what we call a young girl. I ask myself what that actually means. . . .

I read *Gaddafi's Harem*, a book by *Le Monde* journalist Annick Cojean.[2] In it, she describes the underside of Muammar Gaddafi's regime: his harem of girls kidnapped from their families to become his sex slaves. Gaddafi was well known for making room for women in his organization – everyone knows about his famous Amazon bodyguards and how he made them the standard-bearers of his revolution. Each of these guards possessed an identity card. Last name, first name, photo, and the following inscription: "Daughter of Muammar Gaddafi." Bodyguards and "whores," these women were the Guide's daughters; they were forced to call him "Papa Muammar." After his death, hundreds of boxes filled with Viagra were discovered in each of his residences.

Cojean's investigation rests in part on the testimony of a girl named Soraya, kidnapped at fifteen and put into Gaddafi's service. She recalls the following scene:

I saw countless wives of African heads of state go to the residence, though I didn't know their names. And Cécilia Sarkozy as well, the wife of the French President – pretty, arrogant – whom the other girls pointed out to me. In Sirte, I saw Tony Blair come out of the Guide's camper. "Hello, girls!" he tossed out to us with an amicable gesture and a cheerful smile.[3]

Reading Cojean's book,[4] what catches my attention is Tony Blair's greeting, his clearly trivial "Hello, girls!" I imagine the scene in my head. I wonder whom he is speaking to, and whom he is talking about at that moment. I tell myself that not for a second does he wonder who *they* really are.

That's when I hear a variation on the title of Primo Levi's celebrated testimony *If This Is a Man*, written after he left Auschwitz. I hear that phrase, which is neither a question nor a claim – rather a request, an appeal: "Consider if this is a man."

And so, the obvious: Consider if this is a girl....

What is a girl? How are girls made, and how do they make it through life? How do they untie the corset, the straitjacket, how do they breathe oxygen into the doll's body? How do they make leaps, come alive, jump, run, take on the street? How do they scream, live, write?

In the following pages are casts of girls as seen everywhere, in reality or in our imaginations, girls we sometimes no longer even see anymore. Harems, stables, teams, gangs, groups, cohorts, troupes, collectives, communities, series of girls that say a lot about what it means to be a girl.

The figure of *serial girls* is a hypostasis,[5] a first principle stating that girls are girls because they're serial girls. Which is to say that girls are essentially serial – that a girl is a girl because she is part of a series, as in: girls, the girls, the *Gilmore Girls*, the Spice Girls, the Guerrilla Girls, showgirls, girls' night out, a gang of girls.... True, men also receive their share of "boys": the boys, the boys' club, a gang of boys.... But the label "boys" does not refer to age, nor does it infantilize those it describes.

Boys is not a term that aims to devalue those to whom it is attributed; rather, it intends to name a group of which men are a part and within which they socialize. It is a title having to do with masculine-gendered identification in a general and positive way and doesn't concern the way in which sexuality is lived. However, the story is quite different when it comes to the term *girls*.

Writing in the eye of the hurricane of the feminist revolution, Marina

Yaguello, in *Les mots et les femmes* (Words and women),[6] has this to say about the word *girl*:

> We say a girl or a loose woman, but not a loose man. . . . The word girl is also pejoratively connotated (to "visit the girls," i.e. a whorehouse; "street girls," i.e. hookers), while the word boy is completely neutral. Girl is in itself a term of abuse. . . . Even more so when applied to a boy: "You're nothing but a girl!" The status of "girl" being undesirable, a girl will be called a "tomboy", but a boy will never be termed a "tom-girl". . . . And why has the French word *garce*, the legitimate feminine form of *garçon*, used in the Middle Ages without any pejorative connotation, since the 16th century, come to mean *girl of ill repute*, then *cow*, then *shrew*, then *bitch*.[7]

Girl is what happens between *little girl* and *woman*. In a patrilineal society, it's what remains between "her father's girl" and her husband's name. If, throughout time, the category "girls" has played upon both virginity (in the sense of "maiden") and exacerbated sexuality (in the nineteenth century, for example, *girls* meant those working in brothels), it is because girls remain in a state of non-propriety, of perpetual non-belonging. . . . Hence the fact that they have come to adopt this "surname," *girls*, attributed to women as a positive site of identification (in the same way that other populations experiencing discrimination have reclaimed certain insults, such as *queer* and *nigger*). Inside this temporal and social parenthesis, be it real or artificial, resides the possibility for resistance.

o o o

Here, Simone de Beauvoir's words, which radically changed our way of thinking about gender, come to mind: One is not born, but rather becomes, a woman. "What is a woman?" asked de Beauvoir in *The Second Sex*, finding an answer in the very fact of asking the question: "A man never begins by positing himself as an individual of a certain sex: that he is a man is obvious."[8] Woman, said de Beauvoir, is defined not by her own self, but by and in relation to him/man. She is a relative being. "He is the Subject; he is the Absolute. She is the Other."[9]

In this sense, there is an important difference between serial girls and the boys' club: masculine identity does not depend on the club that the man belongs to. The boys' club comes after masculinity and reinforces it. Men socially organize among themselves, sharing identities that are already constituted. Thus, the boys' club does not produce masculine identity; it is, rather, the result of an identity.

Thus, for the purposes of this chapter, I will say that, generally speaking, the masculine exists, without preamble or justification; it simply *is*. Whereas the feminine (and this is my working hypothesis) relies, at least partly, upon the figure of serial girls. Serial girls is the locus that makes it possible to discover the feminine. Serial girls is not about shaping girls as they are; it is about shaping girls into what we want them to be.

What do these images say, these images of female bodies organized into chorus lines, all alike and moving in unison, arranged to look pretty? Is it not a way to dictate where they stand? A way to put them in their place?

o o o

To begin, an image – one that encompasses all the others. Serial girls are ancient history, and this image comes from the ancient Greeks. I am referring to the caryatids, those statues of women in tunics supporting an entablature on their heads and thereby acting as columns, pillars, pilasters. The name *caryatids* refers to the women found on the baldachin at the temple of Erechtheion, atop the Acropolis in Athens. Though they came to be known as caryatids, these figures were originally called *korai*, meaning virgins, maidens.[10] But I prefer to stay within the interpretation proposed (and widely contested) by Vitruvius in *De Architectura*: the caryatids provide a pretext for a story that he proposes not as historical truth, but rather as an example of the kind of general culture architects should possess in order to carry out their work.

According to Vitruvius, the caryatids were erected in memory of the treatment the women of Karyae, a township in Sparta, suffered at the hands of the Greek invaders. After murdering all the men, the Greeks apparently made the women permanent figures of slavery so as to have them repay the debt of the city-state. Vitruvius's interpretation is contested because statues of women draped in poplin and carrying an entablature existed before the period he discusses. However, what interests me here (regardless of the archaeological debates surrounding the origin and even the meaning assigned to these statues) is the contemporary reading the caryatids can elicit.

An architectural reading allows us to see them as the pillars of the building: remove the maidens and the structure collapses. They are foundations, as essential as the building material. Yet, what they are as well, essentially, is trapped. Though they support the temple's roof, the caryatids are immobilized by and within the structure. They are, in fact, imprisoned.

What would happen if we imagined them moving? Were one of them to leave her place, the roof's ensuing collapse would put *all* of them to death. They are dependent upon each other, in the same way that the structure of the Erechtheion requires their presence. Yet, how these women carry themselves – their draped tunics falling nonchalantly over their bodies, equidistant from each other, indifferent to their fate, perhaps even proud and powerful for carrying the roof of a temple – makes it possible to fantasize the other side of the enslavement coin. To go along with Camille Paglia, who enjoys fantasizing the caryatids' feminism rather than studying them seriously:[11] the temple's roof appears to be floating above their heads, as if supported merely by their shared thoughts. Thus Vitruvius's women are not enslaved widows so much as young women free and single; not held captive by their material surroundings so much as empowered by it and by their sisterhood. For these statues stand tall. And they form a collective.

Women-sentries, guardians of the temple. Women of desire we hope to see come to life. . . .

o o o

Like the caryatids, serial girls are structural. After Vitruvius's story, told in Roman times, the Erechtheion maidens' motif was copied time and time again. Today, in our collective imagination, they join all the serial girls, who, like the caryatids in relation to the temple, are one of the touchstones of our social structure. Does the difference between the ancient Greeks and ourselves relate to the fact that in those days there was religion, the sacred, ritual, and myth supporting the belief system on which women's station was determined? What remains of the link between the place occupied by women today and a system of beliefs that comes down to the part played by the media? And is the frenzy of media images, of technical reproduction, any worse than religious rites, or is it not just another mirror, another narrative of male domination?

Serial girls have forever been seen as pure decoration. They decorate: they function as accessories and jewellery, as friezes and other architectural ornaments. These details make the image and give the impression that there is nothing more innocent than desiring what is beautiful: women are beautiful, and they make an otherwise grey reality beautiful.

But serial girls play a much more important role than that. More than decorative, they are central to the social structure; they are universal and essential, like the brick Gilbert Simondon discusses in *Individuation and Its Physical-Biological Genesis*.

All over the world, a brick is a brick: an object made of earth that must fit in one hand. This brick, used to erect the walls of the most diverse buildings, and which might be regarded as the same everywhere, is always both ordinary and singular. Each brick, branded by fire, is barely different from the next, slightly distinct because of its place in the series being baked. Yet this brick, which makes it possible to lay foundations, to build, also has the potential to become, in the hand that removes it from the building and throws it, a weapon against its metonymic institutional power.[12]

Much like what can be imagined about the caryatids, given the mystery surrounding their history and how they were represented, and also like brick, which is at once material for constructing and tool for contesting, serial girls are not only structuring, they are *de*structuring. They are *oppositional*; their image is *dialectic*. If we listen to the serial girls' heartbeat, if we attempt to grasp or imagine the invisible movement or secret animating them, if we lift the veil on artifice, ornament, pomp, and ceremony, what appears is women's place. And this place, for better and for worse, is the one occupied by serial girls.

o o o

Like their sister caryatids, serial girls tell us that being a woman means being *at least* two. Because, essentially, girls are never alone, we must think about their demultiplication. Not only should women no longer be seen only as split in relation and according to the masculine – in other words, as a figure of alienation – but they should be seen as ontologically several, collective. Perceived in this way, it can be said that inside each woman there are not one or many men; there are women, and better yet: *girls*.

Russian *matriochka* dolls nest one inside the other, the largest one containing several increasingly smaller ones, like a mother carrying many children. Here is a figure of female filiation. But in Russia it is also said that inside each little girl there is a woman. According to that proverb, which reverses the *matriochka* figure, what is found inside each little girl is not one woman but a whole series, a whole family, an army.

That is what serial girls allow us to think, and why they hold my attention. For, if they are the actualization of male domination expressed via the mechanical reproduction of girls (which I will attempt to demonstrate), they are also the site of a resistance. Beneath ornamentation lies rebellion. Inside stone a heart beats. Janus-faced, a coin that has two sides, the figure of serial girls itself is at the very least twofold: at once serial girls and serial killers of the identity that we seek to impose on them.

Double exposure "spirit" photograph of girl standing, holding flowers, surrounded by spectral figures of three people, c. 1905, G. S. Smallwood, photographer

2

Young-Girl

In *A Thousand Plateaus*, Gilles Deleuze and Félix Guattari write: "The girl is the first victim, but she must also serve as an example and a trap."[1] The young girl is a trap because she is the becoming-woman, a becoming-minority that can contaminate man. For Deleuze and Guattari, the possibility of exiting binary power relations, phallic relations, is found on the side of the woman and the child. And woman + child = young girl.

Deleuze and Guattari recognize the need for a women's struggle: a politics elaborated in terms of their own organism, history, subjectivity; "us" as women. (There cannot be a becoming-man, say the authors, because man is the perfect example here; he is the standard.) Feminism has to do with the body that is stolen from us in order to produce organisms that oppose one another within the binary thought system. If the girl is the first one from whom this body is stolen (and this is why she is the "first victim"), resistance is therefore also on her side. The young girl *is* the becoming. And all forms of becoming are linked to this one.

In the same spirit, Deleuze and Guattari discuss contagion between the young girl and the warrior. The warrior makes an alliance with the young girl; there is an analogy between the virgin refusing marriage and the warrior disguised as a girl.[2] And if a relationship exists between man-war and woman-marriage, between the warrior who disguises himself as a girl in order to escape the battlefield and the virgin who refuses marriage to escape the role of lady, it is because it is a question of becoming. The young girl's individuation does not proceed through subjectivity but rather through the relation between fast and slow. A young girl is late on account of her speed, write Deleuze and Guattari. Never on time, arriving ahead of time or too late, her youth is defined by this time lag: I'm just passing, I'm flying, I'm escaping, I'm fleeing, I'm becoming . . . therefore I am.

○ ○ ○

A history, or pre-history, is imposed on girls, and along with it comes a future. When they write that the girl must serve as an example and a trap, Deleuze and Guattari present the young girl as the measure of what one must be and do: to the boy, the girl is presented as the (hetero)sexual object of desire, and as a result, he too is manufactured as an organism opposite to hers and the bearer of a dominant history that he will represent and defend as a man. It is in this sense that the Tiqqun collective, in its *Preliminary Materials for a Theory of the Young-Girl*, takes up the expression *Young-Girl*. However, in choosing the Young-Girl as the figure of "the *model citizen* as redefined by consumer society since World War I, in explicit response to the revolutionary menace,"[3] the Tiqqun collective is forgetting the power of resistance that Deleuze and Guattari saw in it.

As ideal regulator, the Young-Girl is, according to Tiqqun, the anthropomorphosis of Capital, and as such, a trap to be avoided, an example not to be followed, something to be done away with. Thus it is necessary to get rid of the Young-Girl, to kill her off. From this perspective, reading the Tiqqun collective's text is no simple matter. Page after page, one is brought (at least as a woman reader) to perform two readings: the first one having to do with the *real* Young-Girl, who corresponds to the consumer of women's magazines, of beauty products, a kind of capitalist and narcissistic seductress; the second one making the Young-Girl appear as a figure, a caricature of the most ordinary citizen. On the one hand, the Young-Girl is a sexed, singular, minority figure, and on the other, she is universal and non-gendered. In either case, however, she comes out as dark, cynical, dangerous, almost evil.

One must wonder why Tiqqun's social critique is achieved at the expense of girls (given that, in any case, the expression *Young-Girl* is inescapably gendered). Is Tiqqun out to get girls, or trying to save them? And, what if Tiqqun is wrong, and *girls* are indeed the Young-Girls once they rid themselves of the imposed stereotype? What if girls are in fact the hope of the social order?

○ ○ ○

"What is a young girl, what is a group of young girls?" ask Deleuze and Guattari in *A Thousand Plateaus*.

Contemporary feminism resists, with good reason, the claim of any homogenous "we" for all women. Nothing is set when it comes to the feminine or femininity; in fact, nothing is less certain than the existence of a bio-woman as a fixed place from which feminism can speak. Nonetheless, feminism does exist, and militants do act on behalf of feminist interests. Therefore, something of an identity remains, which is, if not organic, at least political, and concerns a class of women.

Intersectionality, which is an awareness of many feminisms and of the diversity of bodies, experiences, identifications, and choices, demonstrates the importance of the hyphen. The importance of *and*. As when Claire Parnet suggests that one way of countering the dualisms of language is with *and*, the *and* that is neither one nor the other, nor one which becomes the other, but that which precisely constitutes multiplicity. Replace the *is* with the *and*. Replace identity with alliances and alloys, contagions, epidemics, the wind.[4] Replace the proper noun with a third-person "ensemble" that redirects the utterance not to the enunciating subject but instead to a collective "body" that displaces any subject on behalf of an assemblage. And this assemblage is girls.

A group of young girls represents the reign of relationship, connectivity, horizontality – it is the *and* mode, the power of the hyphen. These are the assemblages that hold my attention. Assemblages of young women who oppose commodification, the counter-seriality of girls who unmake, remake, reinvent the place they have been assigned as mere ornament.

So this is about giving girls back to girls in order to think about the *we* of girls, a we-girls that voices itself against the you-girls of serial girls.

Printemps érable, © Sylvie Béland, 2012

3

Marginals

Virginia Woolf, 1938, *Three Guineas*. In Great Britain, women had won the right to vote in the same way that men could in 1928, the suffragettes' demonstrations bore fruit, and Europe was on the threshold of the Second World War. In her essay, originally conceived to discuss women's sex lives, Woolf reflects on war. And she does so from a gendered perspective, reflecting on women's place in this battle for keeping the peace. Woolf writes in the first-person plural, in the *we*: *we*-women, in opposition to the *you* of educated, prosperous men, with their slightly silvery temples, the *you* of the (old) boys' club. Between *we* and *you*, she says, there is a precipice, an abyss, a gulf. It's impossible to communicate. The *we* Woolf gives voice to is "a whole made up of body, brain and spirit, influenced by memory and tradition [that] must still differ in some essential respects from 'you,' whose body, brain and spirit have been so differently trained and are so differently influenced by memory and tradition."[1] Hers is a *we* that opposes a *you* that has been shaped differently, that memory and tradition influence differently: "Though we see the same world, we see it through different eyes."[2]

In 1938, Woolf sets her gaze on the processions of men of power; today I direct mine to the assemblages that are serial girls, a wholly feminine procession, a double-edged figure that, although produced by an order striving to keep women in their place, constantly threatens to rebel, to leave the assigned place and take to the streets as well.

o o o

In *Three Guineas*, Woolf examines the apparatus of male power, the aesthetics of patriarchy, and in light of the evidence, she asks how to mitigate the inferiority of the female class, how to give young daughters of educated men the weapons they need to oppose war. But, to oppose war, girls must have an opinion, and in order to have one, they must be educated and free to think. Thus, says Woolf, what women's condition lacks is adequately financed colleges, the possibility of earning a living and being properly paid for the work accomplished, the possibility of occupying a cultural space of their own – which means neither repeating men's words nor following their methods, but instead seeking new words and creating new methods. "We believe that we can help you most effectively by refusing to join your society," she writes at the end of *Three Guineas*, ". . . by working for our common ends – justice and equality and liberty for all men and women – outside your society, not within."[3]

In actuality, women are not part of this society, which nonetheless seeks by every means to give them the illusion that they are. Male-female relationships have been deployed in the mode of negation: you will not do, you will not learn, you will not have. . . . It is an ill-conceived place because it is an unjust one, but, most importantly, as Woolf writes,

> societies [are] conspiracies that sink the private brother, whom many of us have reason to respect, and inflate in his stead a monstrous male, loud of voice, hard of fist, childishly intent upon scoring the floor of the earth with chalk marks, within whose mystic boundaries human beings are penned, rigidly, separately, artificially.[4]

Set apart from this society while simultaneously existing within it, confined within a society that never ceases to exclude them, the daughters of educated men would do well to work toward the objectives of justice, equality, and freedom advocated by sons from elsewhere – namely, from the Society of Outsiders invented by Woolf in her essay. This organization, which lacks funding as well as a treasurer, which will organize neither meetings nor conferences, and which requires neither oath-taking nor ceremony for membership, will be anonymous, flexible, pacifist, non-hierarchical. In fact, the daughters of educated men who will belong to this Society must maintain an attitude of complete indifference; neither encouraging nor dissuasive in regards to war, the "outsider" will have good reason for indifference. She will question the meaning of the word *country*, and when told that one must fight for it, she will reply: " 'As a woman, I have no country. As a woman I want no country. As a woman my country is the whole world.' "[5]

The Society of Outsiders, a positive figure of serial girls, refuses all forms of chauvinism and any prize-giving. Girls will let the boys play among themselves without saying a word. Here, to be passive is to be active, writes Woolf, and this secret movement of girls leads them to renounce the feminine function attributed to them as mirrors magnify-

ing the image of man. This explains men's anger when faced with the
risk of losing this mirror, and the importance of women's outrage, which
is precisely what allows them to go through the looking glass and to see,
behind the uniform, this quintessence of virility with his furious gaze,
stiffened body, medals pinned to his chest, and hand poised on the hilt
of his sword; it is what allows them to witness the ravages resulting from
his actions. "He is called in German and Italian Führer or Duce; in our
own language Tyrant or Dictator. And behind him lie ruined houses and
dead bodies – men, women and children."[6]

o o o

Woolf's outrage is total, and she calls on it to state what would become
feminism's rallying cry of the 1970s: the personal is political. There is
but one world, one life, she says, and if we forget this, both houses – the
public building and the private residence – will be destroyed. Virginia
Woolf is not an essentialist. She is not interested in what a woman *is*;
she is interested in what is done to her and, in return, what she herself
can do. She is interested in women's movements, in the place they are
granted and the one they take, steal, claim; she is interested in their
choreographies.

Woolf was often said to be psychologically unstable and sexually
frigid. This cliché, still used today to label feminists and women who
desire women – as if non-desire for the male body and the refusal of
male domination were signs of sexual dysfunction – was promoted by
her nephew Quentin Bell in his biography of her. In it, he asserts that his
aunt found sexuality incomprehensible. Not only did her personality and
her art possess a disconcerting aerial quality, he writes, but when writing brought her to the matter of desire, she either turned away from it or
used images very remote from actual lovemaking gestures.[7] Yet, as Ellen
Hawkes Rogat has shown, Woolf's novels, like her life, demonstrate more
of an asexuality (which, in any case, need not be considered problematic), a sensitivity that, even though it is not focused on the masculine
and does not express itself through explicitly sexual scenes, is nonetheless present:

> Preoccupied with her virginity and frigidity . . . Bell fails to understand
> that she wrote "as a woman, but as a woman who has forgotten that
> she is a woman, so that her pages were full of that curious sexual
> quality which comes only when sex is unconscious of itself."[8]

Still, desire and the organic are everywhere in Woolf's work:

> Her erotic sensibility took in everything going on around her – in Bloomsbury and elsewhere – and found a mirror for it all in her own psyche. The results of such a life are remarkable, even though they have scarcely hitherto been observed: she was able to embody a wider range of sexual feeling and behavior in her novels, ranging from the conventional to the homosexual.[9]

It can be said that Woolf sets the backdrop for a kind of sexual fascism (heterocentric, misogynist) that her work strives, by every means possible, to bypass, to divert, to refuse, in order to sow the seeds of a diffuse polymorphic eroticism and sensuality, a sexuality outside of identity, or as Michel Foucault puts it: *pleasures.* Like *Three Guineas*, *A Room of One's Own* unfolded in the urgency of the moment, like a book where women's bodies rise up against war. A toned body, an upright, walking body. An animated body, alive, vibrant, sensuous, and actively militant against the death industry, which (we now understand) was invented and mastered by the Nazi regime.

○ ○ ○

You must ask yourself: What is the use of this fantasy of female frigidity? What is the point of constructing an image of a woman without desire, or as incapable of experiencing sexual pleasure, or as sexually frustrated? Why parade the frigid woman in effigy or otherwise persecute her to ceaselessly reinvent a womanhood that is inadequate, hollow, abnormal – in other words, the idea of women as essentially lacking, all of it for the benefit of heterocentrism and ubiquitous male domination, the underpinnings of our social architecture and economy?

And what if serial girls wore one of the many labels of this frigidity women are so relentlessly burdened with, represented as hysterical, hypersexual, femmes fatales, over-the-top, evasive, *and at the same time,* cold, distant, rigid, frigid? Like insensitive dolls whose flesh does not quiver, somewhere between Barbie and the RealDoll, between the inflatable doll and the silicone body, women are, in contrast to men, constantly accused of not being *sexual.* And when we finally realize that they are sexual (as in Daniel Bergner's recent *What Do Women Want? Adventures in the Science of Female Desire*),[10] they are seen as animals and lowered to an essentialism based on physiology. . . .

Given this paradoxical female figure, at once frigid and sexually unbridled, my hypothesis is the following: the figure of serial girls is an embodiment of what is really wanted from women (while at the same time blaming them for this embodiment): rigidity *and* frigidity, that is, an unexpressed – even nonexistent – desire, an unavailability, a resistance to or refusal of men's advances.

Basically, what do serial girls – factory-made plastic dolls, toys, and ornaments – say about the desire and freedom that are persistently denied *real* women?

Kayla, Boston, from the series American Girls, Ilona Szwarc, photographer, 2012

4

From the Latin *Pupa*: Poupée, Doll, Little Girl

In *The Second Sex*, Simone de Beauvoir suggests that, as a replacement for the penis that she does not have, the organ allowing the little boy to "assume his subjectivity" as "a symbol of autonomy, transcendence, power," the little girl is given a doll. That artificial toy, a smaller version of the little girl, can be seen as replacement for the little boy's *natural* toy.[1] "The great difference," writes de Beauvoir, "is that, on the one hand, the doll represents the whole body and, on the other hand, it is a passive thing."[2] The gap between the boy whose toy happens to be his own body and the girl who is encouraged to play with a doll seems significant.

Whether or not one agrees with Simone de Beauvoir's post-Freudian reading, which presupposes that the little girl does not play with her body in the same way the little boy does (whether she has a doll or not), what it points to concerning gender roles is important. For a long time (and this is still largely true today),[3] boys have been encouraged to play with toys that drive them to action: tales of adventure, science fiction, unbridled imagination – they project themselves beyond reality. Girls, when they have the misfortune of finding themselves in an environment full of people who reproduce gender stereotypes without batting an eyelash, are entitled to a pseudo-domestic world, a mini-version of the house they live in, where the doll to which the girl-child is entrusted as proto-mother reigns (while the paternal role is not one of the primary values of boys' play). Here, argues de Beauvoir, the doll essentially represents passivity: if the boy, as she suggests, has the chance to become a being based on positing himself for himself,[4] the girl, meanwhile, is being initiated into an existence that is first and foremost for the other. Thus,

> for the woman there is, from the start, a conflict between her autonomous existence and her 'being-other'; she is taught that to please, she must try to please, must make herself object; she must therefore renounce her autonomy. She is treated like a living doll, and freedom

is denied her; thus a vicious circle is closed; for the less she exercises her freedom to understand, grasp, and discover the world around her, the less she will find its resources, and the less she will dare to affirm herself as subject; if she were encouraged, she could show the same vibrant exuberance, the same curiosity, the same spirit of initiative, and the same intrepidness as the boy.[5]

So many princesses fast asleep, white as snow, blond sleeping beauties; little girls are automatically enrolled in an imaginary landscape of don'ts, of waiting and of wanting to be chosen. In the end, aren't girls still expected to be pretty, quiet, and polite, sedate things to be admired?

But girls resist. They often prefer to cut across the forest, at the risk of encountering the wolf, than to play dead. Despite everything, the playground that dolls open up to girls has not been fully mapped. Thus, though they dress, rock, feed, and bathe their dolls, they also enjoy taking them down into the streets and fields, to the beach, on trips, allowing them to see the world and what goes on behind the scenes. Life is not always so rosy; girls also like to be mean, especially to Barbies, those factory-made dolls, all things plastic ("Life in plastic, it's fantastic," as Barbie says in the 1997 hit song "Barbie Girl")[6] that have colonized the planet.[7]

It is said that around the world today, two Barbie dolls are sold every second of every day.

o o o

Contrary to the action figures boys are given to play with, toys that are associated with heroic lives (ordinary ones – firemen, policemen, military men, etc. – or extraordinary ones – Batman, Superman, etc.) and therefore endowed with a mission and action-packed stories,[8] Barbie is, essentially, empty.[9] A blank slate, a generic. All Barbies mirror one another, and they are nothing but appearances and pre-determined roles. Unlike action figures, whose surname we can assume is "-man," Barbie's name is just her first name.[10] They are all the same, yet slightly different one from one another, depending on what we see in them. Barbies are a real hornet's nest.

Some see Barbie as the promise of imagination, and at the same time a liberating contemporary figure because she is devoid of a prefabricated story and of a fixed identity. For others, Barbie is one of the most powerful images of male domination precisely because she is devoid of a story and of meaning. As surface effect, not only as an object but also as permanent advertising, Barbie refers back to nothing more than herself and other Barbies. Thus she appears as pure passivity, pure image, a thing to be gazed at, as revealed by the etymology of the English word for *doll*: from the Greek *eidôlon*, that is, *idol*. Barbie is anything but real, and she is indeed an object of adoration. But at what cost comes the adoration of this woman among women, she who is simultaneously all women and none of them because she is unreal? In her inertia, how she represents an immutable feminine, named, perfectly visible, and prehensile. If Barbie promises anything at all, it is the conquest of the world of women by G. I. Joe.

o o o

Dolls do not represent what exists so much as the fantasy of what one wishes to exist – if not in real life, then at least in the minds of real people – hence their power. How many little girls all over the world have held a Barbie in their hands at some point in time? Harmless toy or patriarchal weapon? True culprit or scapegoat? Is Barbie one of the means employed to cultivate that illness called femininity, or is she merely its symptom? "Femininity is the toxin; Barbie is the scapegoat," writes M. G. Lord.[11] Does the toy create the fantasy or does the fantasy make use of the toy? asks Marie-Françoise Hanquez-Maincent.[12] Is Barbie determined by what the child does with her, altering her identity according to the various games played, or is she filled with the contents of an identity that leads to perverse effects? On her own, Barbie is incapable of subversion. And even when Mattel gets political, when Mattel buys and sells politics or diversity (by making Barbie an advocate for ecology, for example, or by presenting all of Barbie's "colours"), Barbie remains the same: "The will to produce an ideal of normative femininity is manifest: women of all ethnicities, unite to show off your silhouette and long slim legs; stand as one to enhance your wasp waist, your large eyes, the delicacy of your features and that ever-sleek hair."[13]

If, like a stuffed toy, Barbie has the power to be a transitional object for the child, replacing her mother's body, what kind of object is she? Contrary to the stuffed toy, which is a reproduction of a young animal, and contrary also to the infant doll that represents a human baby (about which a child can say, "Here is another just like me"), Barbie is a miniature woman, a shrunken human with an ideal and artificial beauty that for the longest time and to a large extent today produces something that is given as a universal and that must be challenged: a blond, blue-eyed, long-legged white woman. For some, this caricature is necessary for the formation of the child's identity at a certain time in her or his life. But, of course, it is a caricature necessary mainly for the girl-child's identity. And there's the catch.[14] Camille Paglia has said of Barbie that she is one of the dominant sexual personas of our time, bringing M. G. Lord, in *Forever Barbie*, to suggest that other women, meaning real women, are then cast into supporting roles: "If Barbie were Ur-woman, did that make me Ur-sidekick?"[15]

And what about me? Was I Skipper to my Barbie?

I remember my Barbies very clearly: the tall blond accompanied by a Ken-boy of very little interest, and little Skipper, who grew and whose chest filled up when one of her arms was moved. I remember the happiness of unwrapping them and looking at them, the pleasure of undressing them to run my fingers over their cold, plastic curves. I also remember trying to bring them to life in the red and orange jungle of the shag rug in my bedroom. But in reality, my life with Barbie came down to two things: dress, undress, dress again; and have them mime great love stories ending with a kiss between two rigid bodies. The game only ever lasted a few minutes. Bored, I'd promptly let the dead dolls fall into the tufts of the rug. I felt betrayed. Disappointment gnawed at me. A strange whirlpool of emptiness engulfed everything: my enjoyment and my imagination. Angered by the stiffness of their limbs, their vacuous blue eyes and silly smiles, their hair that had nothing to do with mine, I stopped playing with them altogether. I was suffering from the Pygmalion syndrome: all I wanted was to bring them to life. I did not yet understand that Barbie's aim was to inspire little girls with the desire to become a doll, and not any kind of doll: this white doll. As "Zoe Ferron" says, in Mignon R. Moore's article "Intersectionality and the Study of Black, Sexual Minority Women":

> I never felt like a girl. Never really understood what it felt like to feel like a girl in terms of roles on television. I think roles for me were always skewed, especially what we saw environmentally, what we saw visually. There weren't even Black people on TV when I was growing up. The white people were Barbie, and I am not Barbie. I didn't even feel like a Barbie.[16]

o o o

Barbie is a mannequin doll measuring twenty-nine centimetres. Her classic model is a blond white woman with a narrow waist and big breasts. If she really existed, she would not menstruate and would be incapable of standing upright on her two feet.[17]

Barbie was created by Mattel. She is the first doll made for children with an adult body, invented to allow little girls to identify with human figures. Her ancestress, the Aryan Lilli doll, a plastified blond pin-up at once seductive and icy, is of German origin. Based on a comic book character, she is the sexy antecedent (a pornographic figurine intended for a male audience to offer as a gift instead of flowers) of Barbie, Lilli-Lilith the sex-symbol[18] with witch-vamp eyes,

> an adult doll made of flesh-coloured plastic. She measured around 29 cm, her sculpted face exhibits sassy lips, a trumpet nose, the look of Nefertiti. Her platinum blond hair slicked back in a ponytail. Soon there were thousands of them. . . . In taking form, Lilli became voiceless, mute in her elastic skin, the colour of which varied from bronzed to pale pink depending on the model year. Otherwise spontaneous and rebellious as childhood is defined, the Lilli doll had become docile, submitting herself to the artist and to artifice.[19]

After Lilli's commercial rights were sold to Ruth Handler and her husband (founder of Mattel), the German doll became Barbie, an innocent American teenager, a white-skinned, blue-eyed blond[20] who had forgotten everything that had happened in the world: "A change of scenery; forget about the problems and shortages of a country emerging from war. The woman immigrant, the 'foreigner' naturalized Barbie, turns her back on old Europe to discover the New World and makes her fortune in a society of consumption and opulence."[21]

Between 1959 and 1960, Barbie was an icon in black and white: her hair was platinum blond, and her zebra-striped bodysuit allowed her to stand out clearly on television screens not yet broadcasting in colour. Until 1970, Barbie's gaze was directed slightly downward, her head bent so as to give her the coquettish, submissive look appreciated by fans of the "feminine mystique." It was not until 1971 that Malibu Barbie, a gorgeously tanned blond bombshell, started looking straight ahead: because she drives her car, she can no longer have a sideways glance. By way of the car and the feminist revolution, Barbie's occupations, leisure activities, and professions multiply. Barbie becomes a pediatrician, a teacher, a jockey, a veterinarian, a flight attendant, a First Lady, a nurse, a pop singer, a movie star, a disco queen, a ballerina, a model, a princess.

o o o

Many say the Barbie phenomenon speaks volumes about the status of women – the hierarchical organization of women and their outsider status in society. The doll is a screen upon which are projected (male) fantasies of an inorganic and inanimate femininity (akin to fashion models, little girls made to pass for grown-ups, living skeletons dressed by designers indifferent to reality). It's a brand name that relegates women to an eternal childhood while making them the standard-bearer of ideal femininity. Barbie is an incestuous child prostitute, a Lolita that doesn't age. . . . In this way she joins surrealist artist Hans Bellmer's dolls, modelled on the body of his partner, Unica Zürn, an embodiment of the surrealist fantasy of the child femme fatale.[22] Is this what comes of a female situated somewhere between the totalitarianism of hypervisibility and the dark continent of unrepresentability?

Girls remain a mystery, even though we wish we could capture them once and for all and keep them from growing up – that is to say from moving, from *becoming*. We wish we could manipulate them just like we do Barbie. Because, deep down, the ideal is not the woman but the girl, the middle-aged man's Fountain of Youth, a young girl who does not take after her mother.[23] "Go thee and be proud, now, wed young girls, abandon mothers!" as Medea screamed to Jason. Is this why Barbie was invented – this somewhat sexy big girl, bordering on vulgar, yet the size of a baby? And is this why she was given a name nobody is entitled to disfigure? Does Barbie's fascism begin with her name: Barbie, as in Klaus Barbie?[24]

If the Nazi regime's crimes imprinted the Western world's imaginary landscape with death factories, serial desubjectification, and the awareness that some human beings were considered less human than others, these memories are subtly reawakened by the figure of Barbie. The pink boxes aligned on toy-store shelves, coffin-like boxes of plastic showgirl-mannequins, offer an illusion of happiness tied to consumerism's boundless desire, the flip side of which is a boundless morbidity: the dolls' bodies are many inanimate big little girls, of which you can never have enough.

In those who love her, Barbie generates the desire for more. "The invincible Barbie excels at this efficient advertising networking to awaken children's thirst by way of gadgets destined to complete a wide range all the more enchanting that it has no end."[25] Barbie, too, always needs more – more clothes, accessories, houses, vehicles, and friends. Mattel understands how to feed this desire. Barbie is a cancer whose cells never stop reproducing, and this cancer must be fed. Collecting Barbie is a timeless culture. For though we like to say that the doll changes, that she adapts to the times, she remains basically the same, true to what is expected of her. And this is how we love her: Aryan and Hollywoodesque.

o o o

Barbie predates plastic surgery. She is the superwoman that preceded all other angelic and bionic superwomen of our culture. She is Nelly Arcan's "burqa of skin" in toy form.[26] And in the *Toy Story* of everyday life, she has become real. From now on, little girls want to shine like her. All Barbie does is shine, and nothing can tarnish the American dream. Barbie is responsible neither for girls' anorexia nor for their denigration. Of course Barbie is not responsible for anything; indeed, it is not Barbie's image as such that poses a problem, but rather the proliferation of images such as hers, to the detriment of any other kinds of images. If the anorexic model with her disproportionate curves were just one in a spectrum of images made available to girls from which to choose a thousand and one futures, it would not be a problem. The problem is that this image is the only one presented.

Therein lies the reason Mattel defends Barbie's integrity tooth and nail. The company protects this name at all costs and sues those who dare soil it. In a 2001 court case lost by Mattel, their lack of a sense of humour was invoked.[27] For Barbie's father, his daughter must never be shown naked, jammed inside a blender or a champagne glass. She must not be disfigured for jewellery to be made with her eyes, ears, or nose. She must not be dismembered and her arms and legs turned into a bouquet. She must not be imagined as homosexual, nor appear in pornographic scenes. Instead, argues Mattel, Barbie is eternal and must be eternally respected. The icon must remain untouched, because Barbie is one of the Tables of the Law of misogyny.

Barbie is the domestic comfort of the mannequin woman, machine woman, robot woman, vacuum-cleaner woman, dishwasher woman, Saturday morning quickie blowjob woman. Barbie is the wet dream of misogynist kitsch, where it's Christmas every day because every day you can have a Barbie. And organic women had best forget it, or just go ahead and die, for they are no longer needed. Barbie is the image of what happens to women, their invisible and silent murder. Barbie, the beloved copy, the ersatz, the perfect fake, is the blond, white beauty upon which Mattel sheds crocodile tears as crocodile tears are shed regularly on the fate of women, writing the black book of the female condition, to ease our consciences. The wonderful world of Barbie[28] tells us that we wish for little girls to be like dolls, and for Barbie to grow into a human-sized woman, so as to become, with a little luck, even more real than real women are.

Real Dolls, photo by Come As You Are Co-operative (Flickr), 2009

5

Still Lifes

Not much separates a Barbie doll from a RealDoll. RealDoll, Barbie's big sister and the Cadillac of inflatable dolls, is the Barbie fantasy taken literally, whose proliferation is at once seriality, manufactured product, and enlargement: the toy-object has become human-sized; the doll has grown into a pale-skinned, long-haired woman, and we must worry about who will win this competition.

RealDoll is not Donna Haraway's cyborg, nor even the Bionic Woman. She is synthetic matter for men who want to commit rape while giving the impression that they are just playing: "They're very static; they just don't react at all. But if you don't mind that, they're good fun."[1] RealDoll provides reassurance that things will remain the same, like Hitchcock's taxidermic mother hidden in the basement of the house. She is dressed and made-up, has her sleep face put on at night, and is bathed when she starts smelling of fish. When she breaks, she is sent to a repairman, who, after examining her articulated joints, mouth, vagina, and breasts, diagnoses a replacing of her mucus membranes and her joints.

○ ○ ○

RealDoll weighs about forty kilograms. Buyers can choose her look, how light her skin tone will be, the shape of her bust and hips, her lips, her labia, and the thickness of her pubic hair. Supplied with this girl and a tube of lubricant, the little boy becomes a god. He is five years old again, rediscovering his all-powerfulness, without fears of pregnancy or STDs, and especially without having to deal with consent. The value of the RealDoll lies not merely in the quality of the sexual experience, but in the peace of mind she provides, everlasting love and guaranteed fidelity. "We are there for each other."[2] RealDoll offers the assurance that this girl has not slept with other men: nothing worse than a woman who, due to the very fact of her attractiveness and desirability, is already used goods. It offers the fantasy of the virgin, of the eternal little girl, and also: the fantasy of rape.

The more realistic RealDoll is, the greater the resemblance to a real woman, the better the sex (while it could be said that a real woman is a bit too real, that her organicity puts a grain of sand in the gears of sexual activity). A doll mechanic recounts being unable to resist one of his "patients'" beauty. He describes how the doll seemed to come alive under his thrusting body; however, because she was synthetic, she also seemed to be resisting. "The sex itself is almost a violent act," he reports,

> the dolls are made for that. The dolls can handle a lot of physical abuse . . . there have been a couple of dolls that I've had that were, you know, amazing. Amazing. This hundred pound doll came to life. Like, it's pushing back. It's not just like, you know, I'm pushing on it. But all of a sudden it's starting to push back. And it's creating motion and friction and the weight of the product and how it behaves in this manner is very stimulating.[3]

Another owner explains that when he transports his RealDoll and has her "wait" for him in the car, he hangs a sign around her neck that says, "I'm a doll. My name is Virginia RealDoll." That way she cannot be confused with a catatonic woman. Virginia RealDoll, a name similar to the names used by Mattel: Ooh La La Barbie° doll. A brand name, a generic family name, the industry's patrilineality. In talking about it, this owner opposes the doll to the so-called organic woman, as if opposition were possible, as if it were necessary to specify women's organicity, or as if non-organic women could exist on the same level. As if a woman could be a woman without being a human.

∘ ∘ ∘

The doll has everything required to replace a woman: in fact, she is barely different from one. All she lacks is a heartbeat. Referring back to the 1948 Universal Declaration of Human Rights, Catharine MacKinnon asks (in her book that bears the question as its title): "Are women human?"[4] She asks if, in this world which is ours, we women are considered human beings. MacKinnon, a lawyer who specializes in women's rights (and particularly in all things pertaining to pornography and sexual violence), suggests that the answer is negative: "What happens to women," she writes, "is either too particular to be universal or too universal to be particular, meaning either too human to be female or too female to be human."[5] If first-hand reports are to be believed, having sex with a RealDoll means finally taking pleasure in a woman's body without having to deal with either desire or rejection, without having to deal with a brain or words, pain or pleasure, without having to wonder if this body is indeed human. It means fucking a female corpse without guilt or shame. It's about seeing oneself as connected to this inaccessible body, of at last piercing its mystery.

RealDoll is the fantasy of getting away with murder. RealDoll is the prostitute who is paid once and for all, the bride whose services are ensured, forever faithful and forever subjugated. This is why it is necessary to make the link between fucking a RealDoll and making lampshades out of human skin. This is why we need to think about the connection between the sexual relations some men have with this Cadillac of inflatable dolls and the lewd gaze Nazis cast upon deported Jews kept in cages to allow for observation of their "sex lives": a Jewish man frozen, then put into bed with a naked Jewish woman to see if her animal heat would revive him. Dolls are the heart of propaganda. They represent the legions of women's bodies who have forever occupied the threshold of absolute desubjectification and who resist, standing between subjectification and desubjectification in a no-man's land – or rather a no-woman's land – where their lives are in constant danger.

Thus these dolls must be seen as the "supine," a Latin verbal noun that can act as an English infinitive (with *to*), whose root is used to form other Latin verb tenses. In describing the supine, Giorgio Agamben approaches it in reverse, as an arrival rather than a departure point, as a word that has pushed its declension so far as to wind up lying on its back (which is what the Latin *supinus* means).[6] Lying on her back, in a position of supination, Barbie-RealDoll is that radical feminine root from which other women are formed.

o o o

In Craig Gillespie's 2007 feature film *Lars and the Real Girl*, a pathologically shy young man receives a delivery of a large, coffin-sized box. Out of this box emerges Bianca, the RealDoll he has just purchased. For Lars, the doll is real; she is his lover. He takes her everywhere, talks to her, imagines her speaking to him, dresses her, does her hair, lives with her in a way he is unable to with a woman. We learn that Lars' mother died in childbirth and that this dread of causing the death of someone he loves prevents him from establishing human relationships. Lars lives in a small village where everybody knows each other, and residents quickly accept to play the game. People share in his fantasy: Bianca is treated like a real woman, and Lars is thus led to experience "human" relationships. In the end, it's the town's (female) psychologist who, in diagnosing the doll with an illness (the pretext for the doll's long rest sessions in the doctor's office, which serve as an alibi to treat Lars' psychological trouble), permits the relationship to take its course until Lars no longer needs this prosthetic and lets her die on his own terms.

The film aims to be nice – too nice (it was in fact criticized for its overt Christian undertones). It tells the story of a young man who heals from a childhood trauma through the purchase of a life-sized woman-doll. But what catches my attention is the presence of this doll amid a community of adults (women, mostly) whom the film shows "playing" with her (having fun dressing her, doing her hair, working on her style, in order to form this vulgar doll into a respectable toy). And, as in a staging of the myth, we watch and wait for the doll to awaken from her sleep.

The copy is so lifelike that the fact that she does not breathe seems contrary to nature. But what truly goes against nature, here, is the notion that a real woman can be replaced by a doll, not because the doll acts as a transitional object (which the film's script suggests when the protagonist uses the doll to grieve his mother, who died in childbirth), but because what underpins the film is the troubling image of a woman made of plastic. There is nothing less simple than this image, nothing less innocent.

○ ○ ○

According to M. G. Lord, plastic is key to understanding Barbie. Her substance truly *is* her essence. She was born from plastic in an era when this chemical process was considered miraculous. The era of Sputnik and the first man on the moon, the era of the first credit cards – when plastic became a symbol of money. As Roland Barthes writes:

> So, more than a substance, plastic is the very idea of its infinite transformation; as its everyday name indicates, it is ubiquity made visible. And it is this, in fact, which makes it a miraculous substance: a miracle is always a sudden transformation of nature. Plastic remains impregnated throughout with this wonder: it is less a thing than the trace of a movement. . . . But the price to be paid for this success is that plastic, sublimated as movement, hardly exists as substance. Its reality is a negative one: neither hard nor deep, it must be content with a "substantial" attribute which is neutral in spite of its utilitarian advantages: *resistance*, a state which merely means an absence of

yielding. . . . The hierarchy of substances is abolished: a single one replaces them all: the whole world *can* be plasticized, and even life itself since, we are told, they are beginning to make plastic aortas.[7]

Is Barthes right when, in *Mythologies*, he says of the child playing with a plastic toy that he can only be a user and not a creator, one who uses the world instead of inventing it, a proto-adult whose parents give him a bourgeois future in the shape of a toy? The doll would appear to be part of this process, in contrast to building sets that free the child from what is expected of him – a recognizable world, containing objects that are meaningful because they can be named – and where the child creates life, instead of something to be owned. These inventions are not inert (e.g., products of the chemistry of plastic), they are not imitations or ready-made things, things that do not wear out and, therefore, truly do not age: to the contrary, these inventions are movement.

And so, RealDoll enthusiasts are indeed right: the dolls (made of plastic) do resist. But their resistance is purely material, artificial; it has nothing to do with the resistance of real women, resistance that seeks to change the world and that the doll (as well as the man who chooses her over living flesh) wipes out. Dolls are at once living and dead, representations of humans serially produced as if they were already dead, dead women offered as alive and proffering death as a model (and as a mould) for real women. Meanwhile, real women are the living beings who are truly sacrificed to a death that happens every day, and Barbies are merely a sanitized image of that death.

Guy Debord was right: we live in a society of spectacle devised at the expense of women. The problem with Barbie, as with all images of serial girls, is not one that concerns them as such; it concerns them in terms of a world where the image ends up dictating what is called reality. To express it through Debord: "For one to whom the real world becomes real images, mere images are transformed into real beings, tangible figments which are the efficient motor of trancelike behavior."[8] This is why, when confronted with a film such as *Lars and the Real Girl*, we expect the doll to really come to life.

What needs to be questioned here is how images come to represent not only the perceptible world, but also "where the perceptible world is replaced by a set of images."[9] What then is left of reality, such as is brokered by humans? If, as Debord sees it, the spectacle is the opposite of dialogue, if the spectacle "is not a collection of images; rather, it is a social relationship between people that is mediated by images,"[10] and if we live in a society of the spectacle, we must ask: What is the price to be paid by women?

○ ○ ○

If any kinship at all exists between Barbie and human women, it depends on girls, those little dolls who, like Russian *matriochka* dolls, carry inside themselves miniature women such as those that Barbie represents – women older than they are. Yet girls who play with Barbies, little girls as well as artists who take them apart, reveal what remains between life and death, reality and image, movement and fixedness; what remains between the woman and the doll. Girls resist and subsist on the edges of generic Barbieness, and become a war machine. Although it may be true that we live in a society of the spectacle, images are not simply evil. They always carry the potential for revolution.

Tiller Girls, Bain News Service, n.d.

6

Fetish-Grrrls

Dolls have everything it takes to be fetishized, and, as though they were part of the same family, women also give the illusion of being an answer to the childish desire of possessing another human being like one owns a toy, of reducing the other to what procures pleasure. Hence the necessity to begin with Barbie, the quintessence of ornamentation, of the feminine-as-object.

If few little girls have never wished to hold a Barbie in their hands, no doubt few adults could say that they remain unaroused when looking at troupes of serial dancers, those chain-links of showgirls whose existence precedes Barbie but who are part of the same provocation: woman as decoration, as ornament, and what's more, the naked woman who, whether we like it or not, elicits in us what Susan Sontag called the "pornographic emotion."[1] The disrobing of women, their perpetual stripping, is at the core of their serialization. Stripteasers, showgirls, Rockettes, Crazy Horse girls, and Playboy Bunnies of all types. . . . If there is such a thing as doll fascism, that is how it is embodied in reality. Dressing/undressing: Is that not the essence of playing with dolls?

○ ○ ○

According to Barthes, striptease is based on a contradiction: the woman is desexualized at the very moment she becomes undressed.[2] In fact, a domestication of woman occurs through striptease, this non-event, a practice that gives the impression of being magical but is perfectly ordinary. As a result of so much disrobing, nudity itself appears as woman's natural "suit" – her original state, always in contrast with what remains at the end of the striptease, usually the dancer's high heels. Of course, between the Barthesian striptease and nudity in the information age, there is a huge leap. But one thing remains constant: "eroticism . . . as a household property,"[3] the red thread linking dancers, sexy waitresses, and the naked women of advertising. This alluring nudity, which is revealed beneath the artifice, this state attained at the strip-number finale or which the eye seeks out on advertising billboards, the ultimate gratification, the carrot at the end of the stick, comes to represent women's essence. Female nudity is the pacifier, the thumb sucked by the child, the nighttime sleep aid. . . . And if nudity has the power to evoke freedom – that of early humans, whom we fantasize as free of attachments (hence the exoticism, also, of striptease, as referring back to a certain pre-civilization wildness) – in the case of women it is the dress code, a uniform. Striptease calls for movement, dance and gymnastics whose aim is to reveal, furtively, the usually hidden parts of the body: the breasts, the sex.

According to Barthes's logic, striptease as such may not be erotic; it is a staging of what is supposed to be erotic. Whether or not he is right, we are forced to acknowledge that some men (the majority of the consumers of these shows) find pleasure in it. Are we then to understand that what brings enjoyment is the idea of what should provide pleasure – the spectacle of eroticism and eroticized women – rather than women as such?

This is what Siegfried Kracauer suggests about the American Tiller Girls, one of the most popular troupes of dancers in the early 20th century (and inspiration for Busby Berkeley's choreographic and cinematographic work in 1930s Hollywood).[4] Kracauer writes that the Tiller Girls mark out the locus of the erotic without actually being erotic, as the system underlying the geometric figures they draw together in space is essentially empty (they are not a means but an end) – pure ornament.

Contrary to military displays aimed at encouraging patriotic feeling, "the star formations . . . have no meaning beyond themselves."[5] Identical in size and weight, the girls were harmonized so as to perform precision dance numbers in which individuality was banned in the interest of a group ethic. Tiller, then Berkeley, and today the Rockettes and the Crazy Horse dancers partake in this tradition of girls who not only dance together but also, through the alignment of their bodies linked to each other by moves executed precisely and simultaneously, effect the appearance of a figure, prompting Kracauer to say that this is, indeed, about ornament. These girls are ornaments, and they serve ornament as support and representation of capitalist production. And if "the masses give rise to the ornament,"[6] then these girls represent a production chain.

○ ○ ○

Ornament is its own end, which explains why it is an immaterial thing, a thing provided by thought. The Tiller Girls are fragmented, broken up into the various parts of their bodies that serve the composition. In this way they enact the capitalist gesture that aims "to destroy natural organisms"[7] to put them in the service of machines. Hence, the body as machine. That is what girls of all kinds represent, and what women have become: "The hands in the factory correspond to the legs of the Tiller Girls. . . . The mass ornament is the aesthetic reflex of the rationality to which the prevailing economic system aspires."[8] Hence the sense of comfort it provides. Stripped of organicity, wiped clean of their sweat and emptied of their blood, girls cease to be threatening. They are ideal women, smooth and clean; they do not overflow and are not at risk of spilling over. As Sarah Kofman writes: "To make a dead body of woman is to try one last time to overcome her enigmatic and ungraspable character, to fix in a definitive and immovable position instability and mobility themselves."[9]

Given this reality (girls and what they represent), for Kracauer it is not about turning a blind eye and choosing to overlook the mass ornament, nor attacking it like something evil that needs to be eradicated. Instead, it is about pushing its logic in such a way as to elicit what it can allow us to think: anonymity, or dis-individualization, as the possibility of a radical historicity of humans. Rather than erasing humans, anonymity can allow us to counter a return to what is considered natural (a dangerous pendulum swing), a counterweight in opposition to ornamentation, a return to nature as the basis for, origin of, truth in, and zero-point of human understanding and belief (as demonstrated in claims such as: humans are just like animals; women are similar to females of other species; homosexuality is a deviance; etc.) Belief in "nature" is the basis of essentialism and what post-structuralist thinking opposes.[10] The mass ornament says something about our society, and this is what we must try to see if we are to hope for a transformation that would allow us to retain what's best about the mass ornament – this thing that we want to condemn: the possibility of the collective being emptied of private existence, like what Erik Bordeleau calls the hacker group Anonymous's structure, a constellation of variable geometry[11] where "I am only me," which means that we aren't anything special without others, where our acts of resistance rest upon a "certain form of experience between the impersonal and anonymity."[12] Behind the rows of serial girls, all neatly arranged, regimented, and formatted, between the gaps separating them from one another, resides the potential for them to become free of the mechanisms that debase them and, subsequently, return them to daily use, life that despite everything comes back to life. This is when the mass ornament can disappear, and human life itself take on its features.

o o o

Kracauer's Tiller Girls had a German equivalent during the Weimar Republic and then under the Third Reich: the Hiller Girls. Why did fascism appropriate the Folies Bergère? asks Terri J. Gordon in "Fascism and the Female Form: Performance Art and the Third Reich."[13] What is the connection between the orderly display of *troops* and dancers – often referred to as dance *troupes* (in English as well as in French)? While Goebbels asserted the political value of entertainment as disguised propaganda, troupes of dancers made to perform ornamental geometric choreographies were participating in a military culture serving a murderous nationalist eugenics. Evoking the magic of obedience to an invisible leader,[14] Gordon emphasizes the fact that the girls took on the appearance of the images they conjured: automatons, factory equipment parts, wooden dolls, soldiers. Perfectly synchronized, they embodied order, discipline, control, the founding values of a fascist world.

But there's more. As critic André Levinson remarked at the time, these girls are pure symbol, an animated representation of life; they replace the quest for the sublime through the glorification of biology and mechanics.[15] Tracing a parallel between interwar America and ancient Rome, Levinson warns against the pleasure experienced through this parade of sturdy blond barbarians.[16] The fascist reappropriation of troupes of girls rests on the images of health and harmony they generate, an illusion of totality in perfect continuity with military formations, mass gatherings and the Nazi *tableaux vivants* filmed by Leni Riefenstahl.[17] But the difference between military formations and the dancers resides in the fact that the former correspond to a display of power, which they personify, while the latter amount to a devalued object whose sexuality must be contained, domesticated. If, in both cases, there is clandestine persuasion, its ends are radically opposite: as much as the military bodies aim to provoke a sense of allegiance and the blind desire to be part of the national body, girls act as a kind of remedy or antidote to women's (erotic) freedom. They serve as a counter-example (since the role model is familial and patriarchal), and even as a threat (noncompliance with fascist values punishable by imprisonment). The soldiers are human, representatives and vectors of power, first-class members of the State. As for women, they are its object (the fetish): things to be dominated, organized, controlled.

o o o

Consequently, it is difficult not to recall Agamben's assertion, with Walter Benjamin, that the concentration camp is the "*nomos* of political space in which we still live."[18] And that of Milan Kundera: the gulag is "a septic tank used by totalitarian kitsch to dispose of its refuse."[19] Or again, the words of Saul Friedlander, reflecting upon what in 1982 he called the new discourse on Nazism,[20] suggesting that if these works (Fassbinder's film *Lili Marleen* or Tournier's novel *The Ogre*, for instance) are chilling, it is due to an accumulation of repetitions, incantations that produce a sugary-sweet harmony, a vague religiosity, and over-perfect realism – and that, in this sense, they are not so far removed from the ideology they strive to condemn. Such is the grip of Nazism, he says, over the contemporary imagination.

If there is an eroticism linked to fascism, this is where it originates: in the thrill provoked equally by men in uniform who represent power, and naked girls over whom this power is exercised. And in the end, it is in the blending of these two images – as, for example, in Liliana Cavani's *The Night Porter*[21] – that ultimate pleasure and ultimate perversion are found. A perversion that sado-masochistic scenarios play with and outplay. As conscious, aestheticized sexual experience rendered artistic, suggests Susan Sontag, BDSM revisits Nazi codes like a citation – in other words, not using them literally, thus escaping that clandestine persuasion upon which (in its passive form) fascism's effectiveness rests.

If fascism is perverse, it is indeed in its use of (among other things!) beauty and harmony to anaesthetize the masses and lead them into crime. As Sontag demonstrates in her reading of Third Reich filmmaker Leni Riefenstahl's work, fascist aesthetics "endorse two seemingly opposite states: egomania and submission."[22] Relations of domination and submission are staged: the grouping of people, the transformation of individuals into things, all of it multiplied around a hypnotic figure of power. . . . Fascist theatre revolves around orgiastic transactions between power and its puppets, alternating between continuous movement and stasis, a virile *hold that pose*. Fascist art, says Sontag, glorifies surrender, exalts ignorance, and renders death glamorous.

But these features are not specific to strictly fascist governments, periods, or states. They are found in a number of cultural productions, from Tiller Girls and Busby Berkeley choreographies all the way to Walt Disney princesses.[23] This is why the business of Barbies and RealDolls must be taken seriously. Sold as a democratic dream, Barbie is in fact a totalitarian dream. Barbie is one of the faces of this state-fuelled commodification of women built on their serialization.

Photograph by Marco Giusfredi, 2012

7

DIM Girls

There is one startling aspect to Kracauer's reading of the Tiller Girls: his suggestion that these groups of girls may be asexual. And yet these are girls, to be sure, and these are groups essentially composed of women's bodies serving what he describes as manifestations of mass ornaments: these girls all in a row are sheer surface effect, pure vacuousness, and therefore pure object. "The Tiller Girls can no longer be reassembled into human beings after the fact."[1] They do not intend to express anything erotic, writes Kracauer, and yet what we have here are women, undressed (at least partially), gendered, and eroticized as women. If the Tiller Girls are not, strictly speaking, erotic, in the sense that the goal of their shows is to arouse, if instead they signal the site of the erotic, then they indicate clearly that this site is that of the feminine. This was certainly ignored by Kracauer.

From this perspective, what can feminist thinking rescue from Kracauer's proposed reading, something rather more optimistic than pessimistic? What does the mass ornament, when its logic is pushed to its climax, have in its power to give back to humans: a form of freedom reached via anonymity? What becomes of women within this anonymity? What becomes of girls if we forget they are women?

Decades later, his thinking informed by Kracauer's, Agamben provides a partial answer to this question. He picks up on the positive aspect of the mass ornament, forgetting, for the duration of his argument, what history has since revealed about the danger of masses moving to the same rhythm (groupings and fascist ornamentation), whose emergence Kracauer had foreseen in 1927.

o o o

Inoperative communities, disavowed, confronted, illusory . . . the end of the Second World War, the death of communism, the fall of the Berlin Wall . . . all of this created room for further thinking about community. Since its publication in 1990, Agamben's essay *The Coming Community* has resulted in much discussion, as it humbly gives an updated reflection on community that puts Jean-Luc Nancy and Maurice Blanchot's, among others', essays on communism back on the agenda.[2] To what is Agamben responding, if not a certain discouragement regarding the very possibility of community? How can we contemplate community in an era diagnosed, year in, year out, with exacerbated individualism and excessive – even perverse – narcissism?[3] What is left of community in Western capitalist societies today? What kind of community is possible in the world of biopower and panopticism, where subjects are permanently under surveillance, where freedom is all at once a guarantee, a commonplace, and a suspicious concept? And again, from this perspective, what about women?

Singularity is neither the individual nor the universal; it is the *whatever*. Such is Agamben's thesis in *The Coming Community*, wherein he plays upon an oxymoron (singularity/*whatever*) to effect what his friend Alain Badiou calls a "diagonalization," intended to show that thinking can be elaborated with regard to oppositions in a diagonal process that breathes new life into them. Here, the oxymoron generates the idea of a community constituted of singularities that are not singularities, of a *whatever* that is not ordinary: in other words, a non-identity-based community produced through a means of belonging that does not refer back to the identity-based system – belonging freed, as Badiou suggests, from what it belongs to.[4]

I want to come back to that essay, *The Coming Community*, as it is the source of my curiosity about serial girls, and I believe it can be useful for feminist thought today. Throughout the pages of this little book, Agamben strolls through different time periods and among a variety of objects, seeking manifestations of a state of separation from the self, gaps in relation to self – in other words, gaps related to what we call identity. Covering the centuries to construct the paradigm of this *whatever* singularity, the touchstone of what he calls "the coming community," he ends up imagining a community like one would imagine a paradigm: by starting not from an identity base, but rather from approximation, brief encounters, coexistence. What interests Agamben is not the authentic, the essence, the permanence of the singular; his interest is in "the indifference of the common and the proper, of the genus and the species, of the essential and the accidental."[5] This is what constitutes the *whatever*.

Thus, Agamben seeks and finds actualizations of the threshold and the limit, the point of origin of the oxymoron. He is attentive to "this imperceptible trembling of the finite," to how it's "just a little different,"[6] how it distinguishes and assimilates things, and therefore tries to grasp what occurs in the gap between being in *my* place and that of your neighbour,[7] as is the case with the particular encounter that is the experience of love, or between the name and surname given to an individual, framing a space of difference. In the end, it is life that is present where there is this "fascination of not uttering something absolutely." It is life that is born inside that "gap," and that life is what Agamben, following Robert Walser, calls "figure."[8]

What we're faced with in *The Coming Community* is a hunt for figures, an investigation aimed at delineating the paradigm of that "*whatever* singularity" Agamben describes as a singularity accompanied by a void, meaning a finite thing, even though it is ultimately indeterminable and indefinable. Sidestepping the identitary and belonging (putting the *whatever* itself in the place of identity), the *whatever* singularity, if we are to agree with the example Agamben gives of Tiananmen Square,[9] is powerful because it challenges the state not with a claim of identity, but with the fact of being human: "In the final instance the State can recognize any claim for identity. . . . What the State cannot tolerate in any way, however, is that the singularities form a community without affirming an identity, that humans co-belong without any representable condition of belonging."[10]

Humans, yes . . . but what about women, specifically those identified and socialized as such (whether they are biologically so or not)? Is it possible to be a feminist *and* to defend the fantasy of a coming community? Can anonymity coexist with identity-driven activism? Is it possible, as a feminist, to defend "singularity" *and* be the *whatever*, that is to say nobody in particular?

o o o

Midway through his journey, between Aristotle, Plotinus, St. Paul, Walser, Melville's Bartleby (to whom I will return at the end of this essay), and the young man facing down the tanks on Tiananmen Square, Agamben comes to halt on an image of girls, the only one in his book. It comes from a commercial for DIM, a famous brand of women's pantyhose, shown on television in the 1970s, the first in a series of TV spots still broadcast today.

Halfway through his essay, Agamben recalls that commercial. In it we see girls dancing, their legs in full view to show their tights. They dance together to the same music; Agamben notes that at the same time they seem to be dancing separately. Each is in a black dress (but sports different-coloured tights); staring at the camera, the women perform the same dance steps. At times they are in unison, while at others their movements are not in sync and create the impression of a "dissonance." The result is one of confusion and singularity, of communion and strangeness due to the fact that the girls were filmed individually and only later edited with the same soundtrack. Agamben suggests that this vision of an asymmetrical symmetry was synonymous with the promise of happiness, similar to the happiness that emanates from collective gatherings, arms crossed or hands raised as a sign of religious faith or of political allegiance.

Agamben goes back to the freedom found in these mass figures that freed the human body from its enslavement by (religious) cult, biological destiny and biography, atavisms that were interfering with free will. Thus, the ballets executed by the DIM "girls," like pornography (which was invented alongside the mechanical reproduction of images), had the effect of straightening up the body bowed down before whichever god, giving back its simpler qualities: "Neither generic nor individual, neither an image of the divinity nor an animal form, the body now became something truly *whatever*."[11] Merchandise-body, therefore, commerce-body, body-without-soul. . . . DIM "girls" are both the result of humanist technical progress and just the tip of the iceberg in contemporary mass-marketed representations of women.

But this *whatever* that can be captured by the camera and is manifest in the DIM commercial – is this *whatever* created to the detriment of women? Agamben asks about "the subdued, senseless promise of happiness"[12] that the "girls" seemed to produce. What is left of this, and at what cost? Scientific progress, cultural objects, and philosophy have reimagined the body, and more specifically the female body, the gendered (because feminine) body. However, have these discoveries served a subjectification or a subjection? Is Agamben right to assert that what has been "technicised," revisited by mechanisms, is not the body but rather its image?

Following his brief incursion into the DIM commercial (and after this brief interest in an image of women!), Agamben concludes that advertising's glorious body has become the mask behind which the fragile human body continues its precarious existence, and that the "girls'" geometric splendour conceals long queues of naked, anonymous bodies led to their deaths in the German concentration camps.

If we concur with this argument, what would remain is the body and the image, one separated from the other – the real, living body, and the image of pornography or of advertising. The *whatever* Agamben dreamed of can be born by fusing them; it can be "ripped away" from merchandise and brought into the world by advertising and pornography as soon as they find themselves diverted from their functions. It is through these very mechanisms of desubjectification, and in particular of women, that a resubjectification can emerge, resisting the image of what Foucault named, as mentioned in the first pages of this book, the "Ungovernable . . . the beginning and, at the same time, the vanishing point of every politics."[13]

Beyond the decoupling the state commands, the decoupling of men and women, the watchers and the watched, and among women themselves, whom ambient misogyny puts at odds, serial girls hold together as a single body in spite of it all. This is how they survive, individually and all together: through resistances. Flickers of existence, heartbeats, quiverings: girls are "survivings." This is why I want to try to think about what the "coming community" holds for feminism. With Agamben, I want to dream of serial girls as *whatever* singularities that the state does not know what to do with, before it even wakes up, stretches, and rubs its eyes, in disbelief and uncertainty of what it is seeing.

What interests me is thinking of serial girls as a dialectic image – that is to say, as a threshold between decoration and action, image and movement, cliché and invention.

What interests me is how the figure of serial girls flickers, shudders, tumbles, and makes people tremble.

Vanessa Beecroft, *vb43* performance, Gagosian Gallery, London, UK, 2000, vb43.033.ali.
Photographed by Armin Linke. © 2013 Vanessa Beecroft

8

Tableaux Vivants

To show an image and to make it quiver: this is what Italian-American artist Vanessa Beecroft is able to do. Her living still lifes are a response to Barbie and to ornament-girls, arranged like trinkets on the shelves of our society. Beecroft takes the social order at its word by staging series of girls standing still for hours in an exhibition space. Her mannequins are most often naked except for makeup and shoes, sometimes a bikini, a bodysuit, a G-string. In each tableau, the girls are at first standing and waiting. As the performance evolves, the scene comes undone, bodies fall, and the girls eventually lie down on the floor, shaking, frozen, numb. And this is what Beecroft wants: the girls must not hold the pose, they must let themselves fall. The tableau's success resides in its failure. This is how Beecroft demonstrates that the stereotype doesn't hold up. And in the struggle between the becoming-woman and the becoming-image or the becoming-doll, the becoming-girl prevails. . . .

○ ○ ○

Vanessa Beecroft is neither sculptor, nor stage director, nor actress. She is somewhat of a "redirected painter" who has chosen something other than the paintbrush. Her performances evoke Botticelli, Caravaggio, Klimt, Picasso. She is of Italian origin. She is a fan of Fassbinder, Rossellini, Godard, and Helmut Newton. For years, as a teenager, she meticulously noted in her diary all the food she ate throughout the day. Unable to make herself vomit, she started smoking, then playing sports in order to lose weight. When she was offered her first exhibition, she placed her diary in a gallery. This led her to stop writing everything down; once the obsession became art, it stopped. In the gallery, around the book, she arranged girls, colleagues, acquaintances who, like her, suffered from eating disorders and physically resembled her. They all wore the same wig and clothing that Beecroft had loaned them. They were all images of the artist, versions of her.

Of course, the work is autobiographical, says Beecroft; however, she almost never appears anywhere in it.[1] Despite this absence (both as model and, most often, as stage director – she communicates her instructions through her intermediaries and stays away from the girls out of shyness), her presence is felt everywhere. She is the one pulling the girls' strings, her collection of dolls, her army of naked or semi-dressed women, perched on the pedestal of haute couture high heels. Some mornings she wakes up with an epiphany: the girls will have red hair, like Elizabeth I. Or they will all be wearing white, like brides. She will get naked women with an androgynous morphology to pose for her.

o o o

Beecroft's performances are silent. The girls – models, mannequins posing in the exhibition space – must remain mute. Beecroft herself almost never speaks (which perhaps is just as well, since when she does give interviews, her comments, particularly concerning race, are at best nebulous and at worst offensive); her works are not the expression of pre-existing critical content. She provides few words with which to clothe the girls, no critical discourse, neither about the representation of women nor about the domain of art, only a series of instructions transmitted in writing: do not speak, do not play, be natural, be ordinary, do not smile, refrain from eye contact with the public, do not all fall down at the same time, wait until the end. . . .

There are several women, first standing together, then little by little, one by one, crouching, sitting, lying on the floor. They do not touch each other. They do not look at each other. Each one is alone and yet they are also together, silently, like butterflies pinned to a board, paintings hanging in a museum, without the right of reply. Their hair is matched in shade and texture. Their bodies wear makeup. They share the same shoes and costumes. They are ordered to adopt the same poses, to stand straight, motionless, not to look at anyone, to respect the rules like soldiers. They must demonstrate endurance, discipline, commitment. They must reach the end of what is required of them, touch the extreme limit of what the body is able to endure, to see what emerges when the body cannot go on anymore, when it wilts, falters, to see what remains when the dream fades, the dream men have about women, the dream about themselves that women have taken on and cherished. To see what remains when the example ceases to be exemplary, the fantasy stops being a fantasy, and the mystery a mystery. To see what remains when the image begins to quiver.

∘ ∘ ∘

Beecroft's girls are an exhibition, a collection, clones, deportees, Nazis, robots, mutants, a library, archives, a college, a corps de ballet, Moulin Rouge dancers, a toy store display of Barbies. They are fetish-objects, inflatable dolls and anorexics. They are the Queen of England and Botticelli's *Springtime*. They are factory workers and their product, made in China. These girls are shame. Beecroft undresses them to shame us: to make us feel ashamed of being in front of them, guilty bystanders caught in the disquiet of watching this spectacle of naked women, suffering, starving, shivering, uncomfortable. Vanessa Beecroft takes this shaming literally. She exacerbates its logic, performs it to the limit, until the girls collapse at our feet like a human sacrifice in real time. As Miranda Purves writes, "We saw in her and her work a more extreme version of ourselves and wanted to keep looking, if only to figure it all out."[2] Beecroft's work, she says, is "the mirror . . . for our tortured relationships with models, fashion, food, shame, and desire."

Thus, as an artist, foreman, and colonel, or a human version of Mattel, Beecroft commands the girls to stand up straight and stay still. She orders them to show endurance, discipline, commitment. She pushes them to carry out what has been asked of them so as to reach the extreme limit of what their bodies can endure. Beecroft wants to see what happens when the body cannot go any further, when it wilts, when the dream fades – the dream of becoming a doll. Beecroft's girls resemble many Marilyn Monroes fallen from the silver screen and standing upright like rows of soldiers as much as they do little girls photographed against their will.

In her reading of Beecroft, art historian Christine Ross talks about depression, a depression inherent to being a woman (if the interviews she has given are to be believed, this is also Beecroft's claim).[3] In her view, women are inherently depressed. Depression is the norm among real women (a norm evoked aesthetically by the equation between the animate bodies and the inanimate accessories exposed during the performances), but it is also linked to the normalization of women (women are women as long as they are depressed). Hence the absence of catharsis in Beecroft's work. There is no transgression in the work of this artist, other than in the intensity of the performance: the large number of girls, the duration of the exhibition, its requirements, and so on. "What is the meaning of the disintegration of the pose?" asks Ross. "To be more precise, what exactly is being shown here? Standardized femininity? The collapse of the feminine? Women's reduction to the body, to the look, to the to-be-looked-at-ness? The projection and, perhaps, dismissal of the viewer's fantasies? The powerlessness of women? Empowerment?"[4]

According to Ross, what is called "depression" in women is anchored in the perception of the female body as imperfect and incomplete, elusive and uncontrollable. Beecroft's undead still lifes/tableaux are a response to this; what the artist shows is not the achievement of the artwork but its failure, the disillusion.[5]

o o o

Beecroft quotes Virginia Woolf: war is something men do.[6] But what would the world be if it were devoid of men? asks Beecroft in return. Would it be a nice place filled with flowers? What is the world of women, that world she herself has not yet understood?

Beecroft does not answer her question, but she does offer images: on the one hand, images of models; on the other, images of the military. Beecroft's military are to girls what the imperial aesthetic is to fashion: uniformity before the law. A single viewpoint producing a single body. And here, it is Beecroft who becomes monarch, sovereign, boss, general, God. We could say she is rewriting Genesis: Adam is a young military man wearing an impeccable uniform and able to control his movements. Eve is a naked young woman slowly falling off her stilettos. And they are not alone. Humanity was not born of a single couple; it was born of a whole army.

These scenes of uniformity are cut across by a current that undoes them. This is what Beecroft truly plays with. This is what she wagers on, thus inscribing in bodies, in a single gesture, the same and the different. She plays with resemblance and analogy, both in the juxtaposition of similar bodies and in performances that echo one another, but she counts on difference. Though the bodies, including the pubic areas, are waxed clean of hair, they are not all done the same way. The bodies are similar – same size, same age, same ethnic group . . . breasts more or less abundant, hips more or less round, legs more or less lengthy. In certain tableaux, Beecroft displays women of different ages, or pregnant women alongside flat-bellied ones, a black woman among a group of white women or vice versa. She makes use of harmony and contrast, of reflections and distortion. In every case, what the juxtaposition of bodies signifies depends upon the finale, the ensemble – as is the case in a story, or even in a sentence, the elements linked through parataxis draw their meaning from the overall syntax. The relationship remains implicit, unspoken, between elements that, despite the context linking them, must also remain distinct.

Therefore, beyond the singularity of each staging, we could say that the figure of the army is what links boys and girls. Beecroft claims she has nothing to say about men, that she would be unable to stage them without clothes. On the other hand, she chooses members of the US Marines and has them pose, and, since they are used to standing motionless, we watch them *not* falling. What appears from then on is the following opposition: the military men are to the girls what the state is to the excluded, to that naked life that does not really matter and can be eliminated with utter impunity. Naked girls are waste matter, the lives of those who are not subjects, a community of rats. Beecroft's girls tell us that the concentration camp is not something of the past; it is here today, the hidden matrix of our political space.[7] "Camp," a metonymy for History and its events, is there in front of us, in art spaces that, for Beecroft, are not at all removed from the ordinary world.[8]

o o o

For *VB46*, a performance at the Gagosian Gallery in Beverly Hills – a stone's throw from top designer boutiques – Beecroft asked that the girls bleach their hair and wear white stilettos with straps tied tightly around the ankle, and that their body hair be removed. The girls were asked to wipe themselves gently after urinating so as not to damage the white makeup covering their whole bodies. Under the thick layer, like a newborn's vernix, a red vulva shows through, a bloody, high-contrast detail. Like the breasts and high heels, the labia, different on every body, interrupts the almost android androgynous trend, which Beecroft uses as background to stage female sexuality.

In the gallery, surrounded by white walls, the girls are naked. They are cold. They are sore. They grimace. They are sad. They might cry. They are angry, their fists are tightly balled. They are bored and day-dreaming. This is Beecroft's aim: that the girls let go, that they surrender to melancholy and express it, endure it, in silence, that the portrait never cease to change. Beecroft wants the tableau to become something other than what she had imagined.

As the man in this story, so to speak, Beecroft acts as if she were the enemy, the indisputable law, so that the girls do not need a fiction to interpret what is represented, so that the girls live this performance as real, so that the performance engages them to react as women in front of men and make misogyny appear in a palpable way. During the performance, a member of the audience comes near the girls, a tall, grey-haired man, wide-shouldered in a blue silk suit with shiny copper buttons. The world is his oyster. His gaze is lewd. He snickers, and says while looking at the girls: "Where's the price list?"[9]

It looks like a sacred ritual, army preparations, or virgins about to be sacrificed, and the public lets it happen. Watching. The girls wobble on their high heels. They seem bored. They are there, in their allotted space. They are on their side, and spectators are placed around them. Eyes constantly sweep the scene, trying to capture the slightest change. Sometimes a girl moves, shifting her weight from one foot to the other. She folds her arms, tilts her head, crouches, lies down. Sometimes she seems to be sleeping. Sometimes she faints.

o o o

The girls suffer, yet they remain there. They do not leave the scene. If this is a hostage-taking, who are the slaves, and who the masters? Who is the torturer and who is the victim? Like the girls, the audience waits, and, like them, it slowly falls apart, coming undone in its turn. Audience members will never know what had been intended. Whether they leave or stay, they are in a situation of defeat, rendered impotent, shameful, weak when confronted with the girls' image.

The girls are abandoned. Perched on their pedestals, naked before the scrutinizing audience, bodies suffering, tortured, they are there as if banished from society. But waste itself breaks down and decomposes. The banishment does not take hold. The girls are unable to respect the law. Bodies fall, the image melts, art is a spectacle of defeat. The photographs produced during the performance are necessarily static. They will never convey the movement (nor do the videos give a sense of the duration). And yet Beecroft's performances must be seen as photos disintegrating, like an *unmaking of*. Becoming, here, is not an ascent, an advance, but a fall, a depression. It is a becoming that concerns not a state with which one could claim to identify, but rather a state that must degenerate. And through this fall, bodies falling, the perfect image disintegrating, the army retreating, the catwalk falling apart, appears the impersonal, which is a singularity, the *whatever* that evades the law. The gaze attaches to what melts into the mass and yet stands out from it, where uniformity hits the wall.

○ ○ ○

Through their similarities and the mirror effect, the cloning they evoke, Beecroft's girls figure the feminine as what survives and reproduces against all odds. The girls are not only girls (Beecroft's girls, her creatures and progeny); because they seem to be reproducing by parthenogenesis, they also have something of the mother. Beecroft plays on sterility, even on frigidity: the girls are alone, idle, waiting, impassive. But in fact, they are neither frigid, nor sterile, nor powerless; simply, they refuse to be domesticated. They stand upright, upfront, like that young man in Tiananmen Square, deeply resistant. Is this, ultimately, the lesson we can get from Beecroft's controversial and sometimes politically unclear performances (particularly in recent years, and in terms of class and, especially, race):[10] how can we hold on, how can we resist?

Ob stare: "to stand in front of," "to create obstruction" – hence *obstetrix*, she who stands in front of the birth-giver. In their falling, the girls do not die: they create themselves.

Photograph by Kevin D. (Flickr), 2013

9

Like a Girl Takes Off Her Dress

Vanessa Beecroft's work refers to the world of cover girls, top models, catwalks, haute couture designers, women's magazines, and other variations on the beauty contest . . . as many representations of serial girls as are displayed on runways, stages, high-gloss pages. Not only does Beecroft evoke fashion culture, but she deliberately exploits it: she draws from Helmut Lang's images, takes photos for publicity purposes, sets a performance in the Louis Vuitton store in Paris, dresses her models in top designer shoes and accessories. . . . Beecroft's irony and oppositional stance, especially in her earlier work, lie in how she makes use of the fashion industry: a dual gesture of participating in it *and* keeping a distance, of mentioning it without endorsing it – hence the controversy she stirs as an artist.[1]

It is an irony the nearly naked or barely dressed girls wear: they are like a woman's body during or at the end of a striptease. And tease they do. They both attract and reject; they mock. Is there not something of this irony in fashion itself, in the stone-faced models walking the runway as if saying to their audience of consumers that it can't for a minute imagine what is going on backstage? What is concealed by haute couture's veneer of glamour? What happens when the serial girls – which is what models are – take off their dresses?

"If Barbie has such a wardrobe, why is she always naked?"[2] Little girls dress and undress their dolls. Fashion designers create dresses that are too big for girls who are too small. . . .[3]

Georges Bataille's famous line comes to mind: "I think like a girl takes off her dress." Taking off the dress: a classic erotic scene. How many artists have portrayed it? And how many artists have undressed their models? But what is the meaning of this desire to see a girl remove her dress? More so: to see many undressing at once – on runways, in photo studios, on film sets? What do Bataille's words allow us to fantasize? The little black dress, the wedding dress, the cocktail dress, the evening dress, the sheath dress, the summer dress. . . . The dress culture is infinite. And what is a dress if not an object worn against the skin (since the Renaissance in our Western societies) that clearly says that girls are girls? Without going into a history of the dress, it is well known that in some cultures, as well as in certain time periods, both women and men wore garments resembling what we call a dress. Yet does today's dress not focus upon the identification of what is considered "feminine" through the "enhancement" of so-called feminine attributes: breasts, hips, buttocks . . . ? Does this not also hint at a woman's sexual availability – accessible just underneath the dress? When Bataille says that he thinks like a girl takes off her dress, I wonder if he's not thinking more like a man always looking to remove it. . . .

Lift the dress up, rip it from the body, fumble with the fabric to reach underneath, struggle to slip it down the thighs until the hand has access, caress the buttocks while pushing the fabric between the legs. . . . We have seen this a thousand times in our lives or in films. It's always about the dress. And to describe it as does Jean-Luc Nancy: "To robe and to disrobe have the same root (as in *to rob* or *rauben*: originally, the dress or robe would be a garment that a thief has robbed)."[4] What is stolen when it is ripped off, if not something belonging to the girl thus disrobed?

The meaning of the dress might be partly found in what Georges Didi-Huberman says of draped cloth in *Ninfa moderna*,[5] signalling a gradual fall of the nymphae[6] from an erect posture to the ground, progressively plunging into fantasy or erotic abandon. The fabric draped over the girl's body slides off, leaving her naked, only to land (in big, modern cities) as a rag in the gutter. From Didi-Huberman's interpretation of various representations of draped nymphets, I wish to retain the drape's function as what operates the conversion, meaning a place where reversals occur, the passages, flowing, elusive, between the open and the closed, the modest and the erotic, the feminine and the masculine. . . .[7] Like a Möbius strip, the draped fabric is multifaceted, formed of twists and turns, making it impossible to determine where it starts and where it ends. The fold is on the inside and on the outside, one replacing the other in a finely tuned dance. And, following Deleuze, Didi-Huberman goes so far as to suggest that these images of folds may merely be the moulded shape of viscera, showing on the outside what we imagine to be concealed on the inside.

∘ ∘ ∘

Contrary to the Platonic romantic cliché claiming that the living body is more real than the shadow, "it is only at twilight," writes David Kishik, "that we begin to see each other's truth."[8] Intimacy between darkness and light, image and flesh. . . . It is here, too, that we must be able to think what contemporaneity means.

Quoting Barthes, Agamben writes in *What Is the Contemporary?*: "The contemporary is the untimely."[9] After Barthes, he argues that the truly contemporary subject would be so only on condition of a delay in relation to his epoch (and not as a result of coincidence, as we tend to think). Despite being anchored in his time, the contemporary subject would be out of phase and therefore able, when focusing on his own era, to avoid being blinded by the light and instead grasp its dark intimacy. This darkness would touch upon the contemporary's archaic dimension, which would thus be present in the present, indicating that the latter is archaic.[10] The key of the modern, suggests Agamben, is found in the immemorial. With this perspective, what we call "the present" is the unlived part belonging to the past, calling us, recalling us.

Thus, if for Agamben being contemporary means possessing the ability to perceive the darkness of our own times as a matter of personal concern prompting us to think, it is precisely because in this darkness of the past there is also a flickering light, intermittent, furtive, the brightness of a resistance. We must gaze into this darkness in search of ghosts, spectres that haunt us because their presence is necessary to our own survival. Therein is yet another legacy from Second World War survivors: the welcoming of ghosts not only akin to what the Nazi regime made of them when they were still alive, but also their presence today as remembrance, the past's constant reminder as a warning for the present. . . .[11]

For this reason we should remember that the prisoners responsible for handling their fellow captives' corpses inside the extermination camps were forbidden to call them "corpses," which would have acknowledged them as human; instead, they were made to call them *figuren*, meaning mannequins, or rags, scraps of cloth.[12] Thus a thread runs between the dehumanized corpses and the falling-drape lacking a body, a thread we must follow as far as today's fashion model.

o o o

When thinking the contemporary, Agamben uses fashion and models as his example: the clothes put on the girls' bodies, he says, are at once ahead of and behind their time; they are a requirement revived daily to suit current tastes and with which, therefore, we can never conform. As if the clothes had always already fallen off. . . .

Does the *now* of fashion occur when the clothes are on the models, the "only people who are always and only in fashion, the mannequins, or models; those who nonetheless precisely for this reason, are never truly in fashion?"[13] Agamben describes fashion models as "those sacrificial victims of a faceless God,"[14] which brings us back to the Erechtheion caryatids and their draped poplin.

There is just one step between those nymph-shaped columns supporting the temple's roof and fashion models whose bodies compare to mannequins displaying designer creations or window-display clothing (dummies originally made of papier mâché, then out of wax or plaster, before today's moulded plastic forms), just like the other object also used to display fashion wear: the hanger. The top model as hanger, in other words. Holding the pose (even strutting down the runway), reduced to her image, it is tempting to say the mannequin-girl is as rigid as the caryatids, and confined to fashion's temple. . . . If draped fabric falls off bodies to become like draperies (folds of cloth resembling bedsheets for drowsy, sensual bodies) and rags (trash and death),[15] the clothes against the girls' skin are eternally put on and removed, put back on and removed once again. Caught in fashion that is at once ahead of and behind the present, never really there, the girls verge on a near-living-dead state. Yet it is precisely as liminal beings, neither present nor absent, neither current nor past, neither naked nor dressed, that they represent a force of resistance.

o o o

Of course, top models are among the planet's *beautiful people* – whether in actual fact (as is the case for the Claudia Schiffers and Kate Mosses of this world) or figuratively (given the life of luxury agencies provide for the girls they "sell," and the envy their beauty and lifestyle arouse in those who covet them).

And below *beautiful people* remain *the people*: ordinary people, the masses, the populace, what celebrities become when they go back to the street, or what they would be if they were there; but also, more basically, what *beautiful people* are because they necessarily come from the masses, whether as "self-made men" or simply as human beings, in the same way that drapes are rags because they hold the possibility of becoming so. It is in this sense that fashion models, like other serial girls, constitute a dialectical image: an image that is at the threshold between seeing and not seeing, an image that makes its model tremble. Underneath top models are the mannequins, the coat hangers, the *figuren*, the caryatids; underneath the clothing lies a body scrutinized, measured, classified, criticized, starved, a body sold and bought, harassed, rejected, abandoned, raped.

Thus, *fashion model* remains an ambiguous term, something we think of that simultaneously slips away (*se dérobe*), as

> when we want to hear in the word *people* (the famous, the overrepresented in the glitter market) all those from which the *peoples* are, rightly, excluded; or when we want to hear in the word *image* (the medium for fame, for overrepresentation in glitter) all that the *images* know, rightly, to contest.[16]

Photo still from *Girl Model*, © 2011 Carnivalesque Films

10

Showgirls

A number of documentaries seeking to expose the fashion industry have been produced over the last few years. *Chasing Beauty, About Face, Miss Inc.*, and more, especially *Girl Model* and *Picture Me*: so many magnifying glasses examining life as a top model and what it says about women's place.

Girl Model,[1] a film by David Redmon and Ashley Sabin, follows a former model turned headhunter and the thirteen-year-old girl she discovers in Siberia's hinterlands. Brought to Japan for work, the young girl is left on her own in a small apartment. The promised contracts never come through. The young woman leaves the country with a debt of two thousand dollars, to be paid off eventually only on the condition that she return to the country; her return is implied at the end of the film. The camera captures the teenager's tears. We hear her complaints, her desire to go home, to be reunited with her mother. We see her taking the metro in Tokyo, running errands, going from one casting call to the next, a child leading the life of an adult. But most of all, her eyes reveal the interplay of images, where all the gazes cast upon her, all the photos taken of her, have nothing to do with the face we witness as captured by the camera – a face at first wide-eyed and happy, then perplexed, disappointed, abandoned, and, finally, lost. One of the notably bleak versions of serial girls. . . .

o o o

The drama portrayed in *Girl Model* and the film's political position concern the fashion industry's hiring of underage girls, who are asked to pose naked or semi-clothed, suggestively, wearing clothes that are too big for them. . . . This sexualization of childhood – on the one hand the promotion of very young feminine bodies, on the other the withholding of the model's actual age, and the illusory woman the image creates while, in reality, this is a young girl or even a little girl – partakes of a culture of incest, where parental and sexual relationships are confused, even enmeshed, echoing what Nelly Arcan describes in *Whore*: that ever-anticipated scene in which, one day, the client coming through the door will be her father. . . .

Picture Me,[2] a personal video diary and documentary, was made (in collaboration with Ole Schell) by Sara Ziff. Ziff, a former top model, has become an activist for fashion models' rights as workers since the showing of her film and her studies at Columbia University.[3] Ziff and others look critically at the fashion world's blind spots: not only its treatment of models, but the way this intersects with its lack of diversity. A 2016 Fashion Spot study shows that, on the runways of New York, Paris, London, and Milan, for instance, 77.6 percent of the models are white. The issue of diversity, as Angus Munro, co-founder of prestigious New York–based agency AM Casting, says, "without question . . . is at the forefront of our challenges. The fact that there is an issue at all is unfathomably disgraceful. However, steps forward are being made."[4] Ziff herself has stated that there needs to be a penalty for lack of diversity in order for things to change.[5] As a teenager, Ziff was scouted walking home after school one day in New York. She became a highly sought-after model, and her documentary follows her ascent through a succession of castings, fittings, travels, photo shoots, and fashion shows. In the course of the film, we see her looking at *herself* – in Times Square, standing under two gigantic billboards displaying side-by-side pictures of her, or in a newsstand leafing through magazines. . . . And always, she seems to be looking at herself as if she were someone else, because what lies beyond is a life we can't conceive of: girls living in "model apartments" rented by their agency, who travel and work without a break, take drugs to get through, earn a great deal of money and incur the equivalent in debt (because the agency buys the plane tickets, pays the rent and the drivers, spends extravagant sums of money in their name, all of which must be reimbursed), girls who party, lie about their age, remain silent about sexual touching, and, if need be, agree to sex in order to secure a place. . . .

What the film reveals is a predatory industry that consumes models: sexual advances or aggressive harassment from employers or photographers (no matter the model's age), eroticized photo shoots, photographers allowed backstage at fashion shows who turn on their cameras while the girls change. . . . In every case, the sense that models are "living dolls," not perceived as humans, talked about in the third person in their presence so as to criticize their bodies, which, in such a context, remain the only thing over which they can still exercise some semblance of control.

Picture Me makes it clear that anorexia is closely connected to the infantilization of models (their agencies dictate everything, much as parents dictate their children's lives) and the body type promoted by the industry: that of a prepubescent girl. On the one hand, we believe the models are anorexic, while in actual fact, their bodies are of a *normal* size; they are simply very young. On the other, because models are aware of this partiality for very young bodies, they will stop eating to try to maintain this ideal. Ziff's film denounces the status of top models as props, and their role in a pre-scripted scenario in which incest is an important feature. As Ziff says, "It is an inherently unbalanced and hierarchical relationship when you pair a fifteen-year-old girl with a forty-year-old man who is trying to create a sexualized image." Which brings her to wonder at the end of the film: "Why be a prop in someone else's story, when you can tell your own?"

o o o

In eighteenth-century Paris, an elegant woman was said to be "everybody's contemporary."[6] Things have not changed, and today's top models tell us that girls on public display belong to everybody.

This misunderstanding of which models bear the brunt – a public girl is a body available to all – is at the heart of the 1995 film *Showgirls*.[7] Everyone agrees that Paul Verhœven's film is bad. So bad it has become one of the cult "camp" classics in the history of cinema. The film is considered a failure not only because it is crude, vulgar, and outrageous, just like its protagonist, Nomi Malone, and the performance (judged as terrible) of actress Elizabeth Berkley, but also because it deals with what is possibly one the most tastelessly showy places in the world: Las Vegas and its burlesque cabarets featuring half-naked girls. And yet . . . given a closer look, this so-called "bad" film reveals a significant political engagement.

The main character, Nomi, leaves her hometown hoping to become a dancer in Las Vegas. Naive and innocent, contrary to appearances (too much makeup, too scantily dressed, too flashy), she has her luggage stolen by the man who picks her up hitchhiking, and when her future roommate invites her to share her place, Nomi asks at once if she is hitting on her. Suspicious, insecure, aware of the fact that she doesn't know the rules of the world she is about to enter, Nomi Malone is the perfect ingenue . . . except for her personality. Tall and strong, she has spunk. Quick-tempered, she shouts and curses, fights back, rebels, rejects, abandons and physically threatens people. Even though she has to play the ingenue (she's referred to as Pollyanna, then Lolita), Nomi is a "bad girl" who will steal the show from the star of the glamour revue, Goddess, she finally joins (after learning the ropes in an exotic dancers bar). However, at the end of her journey, she realizes that what she believed to be her place in the sun is in fact the bottom of the barrel. For, under the guise of a tribute to Las Vegas ultra-kitsch culture, in a debauchery of colours and glitter, *Showgirls* targets the celebrity culture, the making of stars and the price they must pay or make others pay in order to become one.

"One day, you'll have to sell it," one casino patron hurls at Nomi (on her first night in Las Vegas), after asking her if she wants to earn the money she just lost by "servicing" him. Those words will haunt her throughout the film. What will she have to sell? Dancing or sex? When Nomi is dancing, as Linda Williams points out, it looks like sex, and when she's having sex, she seems to be dancing.[8] Where does the selling of oneself start? When the exotic bar manager gives girls work in exchange for blowjobs? When, during auditions, the stage director of the Stardust casino asks Nomi to pinch her nipples to make them point upward: "I'm erect. Why aren't you erect?" When her lack of culture is sneered at because she mispronounces Versace? Or when the star of the show tells her: "You're a whore, darling, we all are, we take the money, we cash the check, and we show them what they want to see"?

Toward the end of the film, we understand that Nomi has been in trouble with the law in the past, either because she was a sex worker or as a victim of spousal abuse. This is when the cult film reveals its political side: the glitter gives way to realism in one of the most graphic and violent rape scenes in American film. Paul Verhœven may have made a "bad" film, but he was not complacent about the rape issue. Thus, when Nomi's roommate and best friend Molly finds herself in the hotel room of a pop star she idolizes, when he and his friends repeatedly beat and rape her, when she stumbles, bleeding, out of the room onto the dance floor where a party has been organized for him, the film stops being mere entertainment. The showgirl comes off the stage to avenge abused women, and more specifically a woman of colour gang raped by white men.

"Showtime!" Nomi announces later, standing in front of her mirror, looking like a female superhero in her outfit and makeup. She heads for the hotel to beat up the rapist with a few karate moves (not unlike a scene from a Jackie Chan film), replacing the police, whom the owners have refused to call in so as to preserve the hotel's reputation.

The film ends with Nomi leaving Las Vegas and passing a billboard on the freeway that displays a close-up of her. *Goddess*: the title of the show that made her a star, a star that rose only to fall just as quickly. The ingenue is the film's conscience, the one who refuses to pay the necessary price.

o o o

Like any star of a musical revue, like any prima ballerina leading a ballet company, Nomi is the showgirl who represents them all. And *Showgirls* is the film that refers to every *girls* avatar that came before it: Tiller Girls and Ziegfeld Girls, Busby Berkeley's girls. . . .

However, with *Showgirls*, we face post-sexual revolution, post-Stonewall, and post-feminism serial girls; we face girls who are aware of what they are: eye candy, a projection screen for the most worn-out sexual fantasies. These showgirls and Verhœven's film are not tasteless in themselves; rather, they fit the current trend, eternally fashionable, therefore belonging to this age-old past where girls are things to be looked at. The vulgarity of *Showgirls* is simply faithful to the vulgarity of the tradition it stems from; where it varies is in its merging with another film genre: that of female avenger films, in which women avenge rape.

We could say that Verhœven's whole film is more about rape than about prostitution. Therefore, it matters less to know when you will have to sell *it*, sell *yourself*, than to expect that *it* could be taken at any time. . . . This is why the vulgarity of *Showgirls*, its way of flirting with pornography (coarse language, naked bodies in action, scenes of graphic hetero- and homosexual sex . . .), must be acknowledged. Here, the porno signature is not a shortcoming, but rather the mark of the film's political, feminist dimension.

o o o

If you asked me what film changed my life, I would answer *Thelma and Louise*. Without hesitation. As did Annick, interviewed by writer Olivia Rosenthal in *Ils ne sont pour rien dans mes larmes* (They are not responsible for my tears).[9] Annick was about thirty when she saw the film, and what she took away from it was the freedom – how it's possible to leave your life, to live another life. And that's what she did after seeing the film:

she quit a well-paying job to start a business, and wound up penniless later on. What also stayed with her after she saw the movie was friendship. Annick tells us she has a twin sister, and even if she barely talks about it (Olivia Rosenthal's narrative quickly skips over the matter, suggesting that the interviewee did not dwell on it), we understand the difficulty that lies in "being only a half" coupled with the pleasure brought by sister-bodies living as one.

It's 1991. I am twenty, I am a student, I have girlfriends, a boyfriend, *Thelma and Louise* is showing in movie theatres.[10] I think this is when I opened my eyes and when, for the first time, I could see the victim, the example and the trap that Deleuze and Guattari talk about. At the end of the film I'm sobbing, I just can't stop, and nobody seems to understand why. I've often thought that this film made me a feminist, because it was then that I understood the only possible future for these two women was death, that they had no other choice but to die, that their refusal to be victims was a capital offence punishable by death or suicide. And that in this case, suicide was the only way to survive.

It was then, also, that I understood the power of words. Every time Thelma and Louise grab a gun and fire, it is because they've just been insulted. *Bitch – I should have gone ahead and fucked her. Suck my cock. Fuck you. You're a bitch. Bitches from hell.* The insult is what drives them to action, the words that repeat or replace the rape.

Toward the end of the film, a furious Harvey Keitel yells at his fellow police officers: "How many times are these girls going to get fucked over?" In the southern United States, all women are "girls"; it is just a manner of speaking. Ridley Scott's film, however, takes the designation seriously. It depicts how two women, two *ladies*, become girls. Thelma gives up her nice, frilly-sexy housewife outfit, and Louise her waitress uniform and her well-bred uptight cowgirl look. As the film progresses they do away with their lady attributes: makeup, jewellery, hair clips. . . . They stop washing; their dust-covered skins become red like the earth. From now on they belong to a dry, sunny world, a world of space and great winds, of desert and steep rocks. This world is usually the world of men (who, instead, are associated with the liquid element in the film), who end up as notches on a belt, a collection of species, and, as such, trophies Thelma and Louise keep traces of.

The other girls are serial sites: shown on screen as micro-communities, waitresses in uniform smoking together during their break, teenagers sitting around a table, girls huddled in front of a mirror in a public restroom applying their makeup. . . . Thelma and Louise look more and more alike as the film progresses, up until the last scene, where they kiss, twins in suicide, driving at full speed with a neat row of policemen chasing, their pointed guns concealing their faces. Firing squad, machine-men waiting for the command to fire. Nothing less Hollywoodian than the devastating, desperate ending of this film. Suicide is a better option than girls' rehabilitation in an economy that will, one way or another, put an end to their escape – that is to say, too, their future.

It has been said that *Thelma and Louise* is a remake in the feminine of masculine road movie stereotypes, à la *Butch Cassidy and the Sundance Kid*. But I prefer to see it as a survival story, less an avenging than a going forward into the desert to stay alive as long as possible. What happens when serial girls point a gun at the head of misogyny.

Photo by Martine Delvaux

11

Girl Tales

The girls of my generation, and the girls that followed, and others still, right up to today's little girls, have been bottle-fed by Walt Disney. Snow White, Cinderella, Sleeping Beauty, Belle, Ariel, Mulan . . . the Disney princesses have picked up where Charles Perrault left off and nurtured our imaginations even more efficiently, not only through image and sound but through thousands of collectibles. Barbie dolls, plastic figurines, beauty accessories, colouring books, notepaper pads, Halloween costumes, bedsheets, amusement parks, hotels . . . there is no limit to how far Disney princesses can be made to go. As a child, I wanted, more than anything, the 33 rpm LP that would allow me to listen endlessly to the *Cinderella* soundtrack, meanwhile imagining the long, five-kilogram blue dress and wedding veil swirling behind me in their lavish beauty.

Like some kind of space alien, Disney princesses have invaded us! Leading us up to Merida from *Brave*, one of the most recent princesses and the first to refuse her role. She became the subject of controversy when Disney wanted to redesign how she had been originally drawn in order to sexualize her. Regardless of her detractors (given that, no matter her rebellious nature, she remains the creation of a multinational corporation and, as such, an object of criticism), Merida seems to be Disney's most feminist offering: instead of bowing to maternal pressure aiming to make a married woman out of her, Merida rebels, resists the fate awaiting her, and reinvents her relationship with her wild mother (who is turned into a bear, imperilled, freed from the curse, and finally changed forever). For once, a princess desires something other than pretty clothes and a charming prince, and a mother is not reduced to a "stepmother" role, wicked, cruel, and controlling, a mother for whom her daughter is nothing but a threat, a thing to humiliate or abandon so as to preserve her own power.[1]

But Snow White, Cinderella, Ariel – such are the more traditional heroines Disney serves up to little girls. And there is the latent content that movies like *Showgirls* and *Thelma and Louise* stand against, as do *Hard Candy* and *The Brave One*[2] – they are rereadings, via the revenge film, of Little Red Riding Hood.

o o o

In line with *Taxi Driver*'s Travis Bickle, Hayley Stark (Ellen Page) and Erica Bain (Jodie Foster), the heroines of *Hard Candy* and *The Brave One*, respectively,[3] take justice into their own hands, avenging girls and women by giving pedophiles, pimps, hoodlums, rapists, and serial killers what they deserve. Where Travis Bickle was driven by uncontrollable violent urges due to his maladjustment and what the script presents to us as a form of insanity (a consequence of his military experience in Vietnam), Hayley Stark and Erica Bain appear to be people with a conscience and a moral compass. They refuse to consent, to learn the lesson of suffering and terror seemingly imposed on them; they disobey society's unwritten rules that girls, women, are essentially victims. Here, distress does not cause anaesthesia (medicalized or not); rather, it triggers actions that, beyond the survival of the woman performing them, aim to protect and avenge others like herself. In these films, the neighbourhood watch is more than some kind of passive surveillance; it means taking real action. Hayley Stark and Erica Bain hunt down and punish criminals, like an alternate version of Little Red Riding Hood where she ends up trapping the wolf and keeping him from attacking others.

Fairy tales say the following: little girls must be sweet and nice, passive, submissive, mute, destined to lay in wait, and, especially, obedient. Is this not what Charles Perrault writes at the end of his *Little Red Riding Hood*? Young girls, "attractive, well bred young ladies, should never talk to strangers."[4] Girls are the daughters of their fathers, of father-justice, father-law, and when choosing between him and the worst-case scenario, they must always choose him. But what if, as Catherine Orenstein suggests,[5] Little Red Riding Hood and the wolf were two aspects of the same subject, that by operating as a parallax, Little Red Riding Hood and the wolf appeared as two different and irreconcilable (yet interwoven) perspectives on the same object? And what if this sweet and innocent girl was, basically, the wolf – what if instead of enjoying her role as a submissive little girl she chose to occupy her place, to let him devour her so she could live inside him, evict him, steal his skin? She would then become both beauty and the beast. She would no longer be Donkeyskin

(*Peau d'âne*)[6] but Wolfskin (*Peau de loup*). And what would this mean for the power (the anger, rage, revenge) of women?

o o o

Hard Candy and *The Brave One* echo Perrault's tale: the red hoodie Hayley Stark wears at the beginning of the movie and which she soon removes, only to put back on at the very end, once the pedophile has committed suicide; Erica Bain's wolf-dog, used by her attackers to draw her and her fiancé into a trap (the animal is freed at the end, once the ultimate revenge has been perpetrated upon the assailants); the cross-dressing by the protagonists, who swiftly exchange skirts for pants (and, in Hayley Stark's case, a surgeon's scrubs); Hayley Stark's visit to the pedophile's house, which appears isolated though it is located right in the city and whose square shape is constantly emphasized (the camera frames walls where paintings are hung), thus conceptualizing ad infinitum how the core components of Perrault's tale dovetail into one another,[7] as if the screen were the pages of an illustrated children's book; and finally, the walk taken by Erica Bain through the streets of nighttime New York, like Little Red Riding Hood walking through the forest. . . . All of these recall the fairy tale.

If seeing the wolf means losing one's virginity, *Hard Candy* and *The Brave One* tell the story of innocence lost at the hands of violence: a friend's disappearance and a bitter awareness of pedophilia, for Hayley Stark; and for Erica Bain, surviving an attack during which her fiancé is killed. "How do you keep on living once you have seen the wolf?" these films ask. As for Hayley Stark and Erica Bain, they become vigilantes because they have learned to decode the world and make their mark on it. If they dance with the wolves, it is with the intention of killing them, paying back in kind those who devour little girls.[8]

o o o

In both films, the man utters the same threat: "You ever been fucked by a knife?" (*The Brave One*); "Which do you want to fuck first, me or the knife?" (*Hard Candy*). Against the knife/phallus that is the rapist-wolf's tool, and against those who use it to subjugate women, the heroines make use of a computer (word processor, chat, and email), a scalpel (medical techniques), a gun (police techniques), a cellphone (communication device). . . .

Hayley to Jeff: "I mean, you really got to start to wonder when a grown man goes through all this trouble just to charm a girl. Wow. There's that word again. 'Girl.' You know, maybe it's this whole camera thing? Cameras, computers. They let you hide, don't they? So safe. I heard how your voice changed when the camera came between us."

The ordinary woman turns out to be a terrorist who inverts the objects used by the whole wolf-system to dominate her. Contrary to Little Red Riding Hood being swallowed by the wolf (and who is freed by a hunter in the Brothers Grimm's version),[9] here Little Red Riding Hood seems to have swallowed the beast, revealing that she may have been carrying him inside her all along.

For Peter Sloterdijk, modern times are the era of monstrosities created by man. "To be modern, one must be touched by the awareness that, beside the inevitable fact of being a witness, one has been drawn into a sort of complicity with the newer form of the monstrous."[10] At the moment of the crime, the modern individual finds her or himself at the scene of the crime. She or he is not an innocent bystander, she or he has no alibi.[11] Is this not Erica Bain's experience after her assault, as she discovers her inner "monster"? Like an organism mutating in order to adapt to a new environment, it is this monster, produced in reaction to the assault, that from now on makes her act and speak out as a witness.

o o o

The Brave One opens with a woman's voice as she wanders through New York via radio waves: "I'm Erica Bain. And as you know, I walk the city." After leaving the hospital and trying to resume a normal life following her assault and the murder of her fiancé, she happens to witness another murder: one night, while buying milk in a convenience store, she sees a man killing his wife, the cashier, because she refuses him access to their children. When the man notices Erica, he starts chasing after her, attacks her, and to protect herself she pulls out her gun, fires, and kills him.

Describing her transformation after experiencing her fear, her new perception of the city, Erica declares over the airwaves: "Inside you there is . . . a sleepless, restless stranger who keeps walking, keeps eating, keeps living." Later on, when a policeman asks how she was able to get over her attack, she answers: "You don't. . . . You become someone else. A stranger." Like the wolf disguised as the grandmother, Erica cross-dresses – "Hey, you," she says harshly to her image in the mirror. She seems to be wearing a uniform, somewhere between policeman and soldier, setting aside skirts and camisoles for black pants and T-shirts. To find her, the police must forego their usual logic ("Women kill . . . shit they love. They don't do this.") They soon start looking for "a woman who wants revenge."

Erica Bain's transformation could be summarized as a shift from first person to second person. It is the parallax of the "you," that double-faced pronoun she uses all the time. Both an engine of subjectification and desubjectification, the "you" is a kind of quotation: Erica Bain claims the crime so that justice may be carried out. She follows the other's movements inside herself in the same manner as she walks through the streets of New York, tracking down the monsters threatening her species. The alien is not an alibi; it is the means of carving out a different place[12] for oneself and defending the place of all women.

o o o

In a similar manner, Hayley Stark's character in *Hard Candy* merges with an unidentified group of faceless girls, all of them known or potential victims of pedophilia: "I am every little girl you ever watched. Touched. Hurt. Screwed. Killed. . . ." Hayley Stark plays the game of anonymity, of the little girl fallen into the big bad wolf's trap to call up the ghosts of the girls who have disappeared or who are in danger. As though girls were an endangered species, needing to be protected from predators.

The heroine of *Hard Candy* dresses as Little Red Riding Hood to conceal the wolf she carries inside herself, like a monster confronting another monster that refuses to admit what it really is – Jeff the pedophile: "I'm not the monster you think." Though Jeff attempts to convince her of his innocence, Hayley Stark is no fool. She refuses to listen, tortures him, shames him to the point where he commits suicide. Not only does she interrupt him constantly so as to silence him for good, but she also possesses the power to reply, to manipulate words, sentences, and critical theory.

Jeff the pedophile produces images (he claims to be a photographer), and Hayley Stark produces words. It is with words that she defeats him and the images he produces, in the same way that Erica Bain duplicates her gestures of violence by commenting on them over the radio, thus making public (all the while keeping them secret) her vigilante actions. Therein lies the specificity of these two lawmakers: they leap into action, and this move to action is coupled with a relationship to discourse and to story-making. They play these roles concurrently and become all at once the wolf, Little Red Riding Hood, and author Charles Perrault himself. Their power resides in refusing the victim stance prescribed by the ambient discourse, which, obeying a perverse logic, decries violence against women with the goal not of protecting them, but of silencing them.

The wolf-woman must be seen as what becomes of Little Red Riding Hood, not because she has not fully learned her lesson but because the lesson was a lure, a way of grooming its victims.

Photo by Éléonore Delvaux-Beaudoin and Martine Delvaux, Barbie expo, Les Cours Mont-Royal, Montreal

12

One for All, All for One

To live or die, or perhaps to be or not to be, to be in such a way that it will not be the last time. . . . Those are the issues that thread through the struggle between a Little Red Riding Hood and the "Once upon a time" that seals her entry into literature. All little girls, all fairy-tale princesses are, at some point, victims. The "Once upon a time" is a lie: basically, what these words mean is "Once upon a time, and there will be many more times, indefinitely, till the end of time."

Serial girls are a phenomenon of repetition. The girls are multiple, they are serial, and so is the series that they form. Everywhere, girls, together, looking alike. The lawmakers are what fairy-tale girls become when they suddenly take on the role of superheroines. They are politicized serial girls who find, in not being only one, the strength to be a collective. When a girl splits off from the series, it is sometimes to express herself on behalf of all the others. She refuses to be the exception and remains faithful to the group, making her body and her voice vibrate with the inflections of the women she carries within herself, representing them like a flag, the mask of a woman whose name, in the end, does not matter. For in serial girls resides the power of a *how* that unfolds in place of the identity-based *who* that seriality gives rise to, that ornamental mask imposed on women as though it were an identity.

Thus, if one of them cuts off from the mass, all of the girls start to exist, the singular voice put into the service of an anonymity that is a political force. It is not just about speaking for others, but rather, as Deleuze wrote, about "naming the impersonal, physical and mental powers which we face and fight as soon as we attempt to reach a goal, and that we do not lose sight of this goal only during the struggle."[1] It follows that "power becomes biopower, resistance becomes the power of life."[2]

In *Foucault anonymat* (Foucault anonymity), Erik Bordeleau shows that, for Foucault, anonymity is not about playing anonymity against identity as much as it is about problematizing the processes of subjectification stemming from our relationships with apparatuses.[3] And serial girls are indeed an apparatus, what Agamben describes as "anything that has in some way the capacity to capture, orient, determine, intercept, model, control, or secure the gestures, behaviors, opinions or discourses of living beings."[4] His classification includes not only prisons, schools, asylums, factories, legal measures . . . the many faces of the panopticon whose intersecting points with power are obvious, but also ballpoints, writing, literature, philosophy, computers, cigarettes, cellphones, even language itself. According to Agamben, there are living beings on one side, and apparatuses on the other. And between the two, the processes of subjectification can emerge. Therefore, it is not possible simply to claim that the living are alienated by apparatuses. Instead, it is important to see that the living can always strike a balance by desecrating the apparatus, until we arrive at the point where "nothing looks more like a terrorist than the ordinary man."[5]

An ordinary *man*? Or rather: a *woman*.

○ ○ ○

It is 1980, in East Germany. Because she sought to escape to the West, a woman named Barbara is forced by the state to leave Berlin for a little town near the Baltic Sea. We understand that she has been imprisoned. This move is punishment in the form of deportation. Barbara is a doctor. She leaves the prestigious Charité hospital to practice in a rural hospital, under surveillance by the Stasi, represented by a policeman and by the chief physician, André. With the latter, she ultimately develops a relationship, an intimacy with romantic overtones founded on shared work. Although it seems to form the core of the movie, this romantic subplot is something of a false lead.

Barbara:[6] actress Nina Hoss, director Christian Petzold's muse, plays the part of this woman at the centre of a hostile world, an island-like seaside penitentiary from which she initially seeks to escape. Rather silent, tall and upright, cold and emotionless, her huge eyes, her mesmerizing gaze, devour the screen. She is filmed in close-ups, often alone onscreen, as if caught in the camera's net: if the title of Petzold's film is a woman's name, it is because she is the one who concerns us, who looks at us: "I wanted to only film personal gazes," says Petzold, "how people look at each other. Looking and being looked at."[7]

Petzold burdens a woman, and maybe even only her face, maybe even only her given name, with much more than an identity. It is like in Rembrandt's 1632 painting *The Anatomy Lesson of Dr. Nicolaes Tulp*, which

André, the chief physician, comments on in his attempt to seduce Barbara. A thief has just been hanged, his autopsy is being performed, the seven surgeons present are all staring at the enormous textbook lying open at the cadaver's feet. But something in this painting is jarring: the dissected left hand turns out to be the right hand, and is out of proportion with the rest of the body. This error, André explains to Barbara, is no mistake; it is a strategy used to encourage viewers to look at the victim rather than at the doctors. This is what Petzold does in his film as well: he invites us to look at Barbara rather than the representatives of power.

o o o

To start, the opening scene: from a hospital window, from the same viewpoint as the chief physician and the Stasi agent, we see Barbara sitting on a bench, smoking. We also hear the Stasi agent telling the doctor who he is. We understand that both men are meant to keep an eye on her. This is the only time she is seen from above, from the viewpoint of those watching her. Then, leaving the heights, we find ourselves at ground level, with her, up close, much like Stella, the young girl Barbara takes in her arms or hugs against her body several times during the film.

Stella's character recalls Aris Kindt, the hanged thief in the Rembrandt painting. This young girl, who is pregnant, routinely escapes from the labour camp where she has been sent. This time around she has fled through fields and, in doing so, has caught meningitis. As soon as she arrives at the clinic, Barbara starts caring for her. First she asks the policemen to stop violently restraining her, then she speaks to her gently: "Stella . . . Stella . . ." Later on, when André refers to "the girl," Barbara corrects him: "Stella. The girl's name is Stella." In fact, Stella also names Barbara, *calls her*, deepening intimacy and identification by shifting from "Frau Doktor" to the proper name she pronounces softly so as to draw her closer, and which she ends up screaming when guards arrive to return her to the camp.

Barbara is a portrait of a woman torn between trust and distrust, like she is between the GDR (German Democratic Republic) and the FRG (Federal Republic of Germany). Trapped, too, between herself and others – the girls and the women who, one way or another, reflect her image back to her. Thus, like Stella, despite having been found guilty and punished, Barbara continues to be defiant. And like the corpse in *The Anatomy Lesson*, which we gaze at as if it could still breathe, we see

Barbara as the one who refuses to stop fighting. She always carves out a space for freedom in her open-air prison. The back-and-forth between the shoddy apartment where she is forced to live and the medical clinic where she has to work, her multiple bicycle treks to meet up with her secret lover, up until the final trip to the seashore – Barbara is always in motion. While Stella repeatedly runs across fields to flee Torgau, Barbara rides a bicycle.

o o o

At the end of *A Woman in Berlin*,[8] Nina Hoss (who plays the lead in this film as well) rides across the city, and across the screen, on a bicycle that represents what remains of freedom in a world where German women of all ages have become bodies to be raped, serial girls in a merciless war. . . . Adapted from the diary kept by a journalist during the Red Army's occupation of the capital, the movie bears witness to the systematic rape of the women of Berlin as Soviet soldiers took revenge for the massacres committed in their country.

There is a connection between *A Woman in Berlin* and *Barbara*, a similar way of occupying space to imprint it with a woman's life: perpetual movement, which, in *Barbara*, contrasts with what the lover from the West describes as her future life. In fact, he offers up a cliché that FRG men often catered to GDR women, which inspired Petzold's work: "I earn enough money, you won't have to work." East German women were part of the workforce and, once on the other side of the wall, they had the misfortune to find themselves in a domestic prison worse than their jobs under the Communist regime. Thus, all the women Barbara meets are workers: the concierge, the restaurant waitresses (stretched out on the floor, buttocks against the wall and legs up at a right angle, like inverted dancing girls), the doctors and nurses, even the Olympic medalist mentioned on the radio.

It is once she comes into contact with these women that Barbara begins to waver. Her aloofness softens; she allows herself to be touched by those she meets and cares for, who call for her and to whom she responds. These girls and women are the reverse of the monitoring gaze. Though Barbara is isolated, she is not isolated from them. We could even say that Barbara is a metonymy for all women, that in itself her name harbours the destiny of all women and girls: the little hospitalized girl in the pediatric room who screams in her sleep, the teenage girl visiting her boyfriend who has just attempted suicide, Steffi (the young mistress of Barbara's lover's friend, who has been promised marriage and passage to the West), and finally, Stella. In yielding her place to Stella in the small boat that was to illegally carry her to Denmark, and her lover, Barbara chooses not to leave the GDR. She chooses to remain as close as possible to all of these women, to live with them and, like them, to be part of the series. And in one of the film's final scenes, for one last time we hear the name Barbara being screamed out by Stella as she disappears over the horizon aboard the clandestine boat.

o o o

In his *Theory of Proper Names*, Alan Gardiner suggests that what defines a proper name is its sound, the fact that there is a basic, direct relation between an individual and her or his name.[9] The name matters because it inscribes the individual in reality, hence the importance of monuments that consist of lists of names, as in memorials to victims of Nazi deportations or AIDS. Naming has to do with being brought into this world. We baptize, we inaugurate, we name: the name confers existence.

In a patrilineal regime, women, when they marry, must exchange or choose to exchange their father's name for their husband's, or to give the latter to their children. But the surname is not the only name that matters. As Marina Yaguello indicates, we must also tackle the question of the given name.[10] On the one hand, women can find themselves identified by their husband's full name and see their own given name swallowed by his (as in the example she gives of Mrs. John Y.). On the other hand, they can be identified by their given name alone, leaving it to men to wear a full name (as is often the case for women writers, whom we tend to identify by their first name only: Marguerite, Virginia . . .).

"There exists an obvious relation between power and the right to name,"[11] writes Yaguello, just like there is an obvious link between the right to be adequately named and a form of power that is granted to us. Yaguello notes the trend[12] of giving girls names that are considered "feminine" – the names of flowers, Christian festive events, abstract values, as well as given names that are diminutives. Thus, she concludes, "it is by giving herself a name that does not reflect her social status that a woman can conquer her social identity and her identity as such. For now, she has no name and therefore no voice."[13]

o o o

If the personal is political, it is via the given name that, as with Petzold, the equation balances out. The given name Barbara, a quasi-palindrome given its mirror-like spelling, is at once the name of a woman and the name of all the women who begin to exist thanks to her, with and through her. That is to say, through the film's perception of women, the viewpoint it invites us to share, asking us, first and foremost, to see *them.*

Barbara recalls Cassavetes' Gloria as well as other women from film history – Vera Drake, Frances Farmer, Norma Rae, Erin Brockovich, and, more recently, Frances Ha. She also brings to mind all the nameless girls in the work of Québécoise poet Josée Yvon, who wrote, "for all the operators named Lise working at Bell, all the Dianes murdered at Simpson's Sears, the Jayne Mansfields raped as they were leaving school."[14]

Yvon's poetry abounds with girls named Micheline, Ginny, Lucienne, Nancy, Jackie, Nicole, Nanette, Eugénie Jones, Thérèse the redhead, Denise the lil' shit, Patsy from Sainte-Monique, long tall Caouette, Aline Duchesneau, shorty Maltais from Saint-Wilbrod. . . . With her poetry, the belly of the Trojan horse opens upon a community of "missile-girls" whose names are like sparks, flashlight beams ushering the way through the violent movie of daily life and of revolution.

"Filles du ciel et de la mort" (girls of heaven and of death), *"filles percées comme des perles"* (girls pierced like pearls), *"blessées d'hiver"* (winter wounded women)[15] – Josée Yvon saves nameless girls by retrieving them into memory. These girls are part of the pantheon of the forgotten, a series of women fallen through the social fabric, harassed, depressed, damaged, in the image of Marguerite Duras' various pale, evanescent Lol V. Steins, which, when reversed, shows the face of the women-witches who inhabit her film *Nathalie Granger,* women, cloaked in black, who resist the conjugal and domestic space, move into the forest, chase men away, and choose to remain only with each other.

The nameless girls also conjure up the 1,653 quotes collected, orchestrated, and edited by French author Eléonore Mercier in her book *Je suis complètement battue* (I am completely battered).[16] These 1,653 first sentences were recorded while she was working for a helpline for women victims of domestic violence, and from them, life stories are imagined, reconstructed by readers who find themselves in the grip of, in this case, the book. The sentences, edited like a movie made by an invisible director, resonate like a faceless choir. Like a desperate refrain of violence, each one of these sentences can be read like a body blow.

And what is left of these Jane Does is a pronoun, an utterance, an address: from now on, *we* are the ones at the other end of the phone. In *Je suis complètement battue*/I am completely battered, the *I* is anonymous. And this anonymity gives rise to a community: one obviously made up of pain, but also one of a potential resistance that is left in the reader's hands. We are the witnesses asked to carry the images and recognize ourselves in them, just like a mirror.

○ ○ ○

In 2013, a commercial (titled "Jedna fotografija dnevno u najgoroj godini života / One photograph a day during the worst year of my life") went viral on the web and social media via YouTube (where it was posted anonymously on March 18). A woman takes a photo every day throughout one year, photo-documenting her transformation into a "battered woman." In the last take, we see her holding up a small poster that says, in Serbian: "I don't know if I can hold out until tomorrow." Mise en scène and montage, one way of making a lot of noise with minimal means,[17] this video is striking due to the transformation it portrays – not only because of the visible traces of violence that appear as the images unfold, but also because each face seems to belong to a different woman. Behind this "lone" woman, the video allows us to think (imagine?) that there may be hundreds, thousands of others, an infinite number of battered women, terrorized, murdered by men with whom they share or have shared their lives.

Beyond this video, or perhaps alongside it, at the same moment, in the winter of 2013, we find (little) girls raped and murdered in India, young students in Steubenville and Halifax drugged, raped, and driven to commit suicide, Aboriginal women disappeared in the Downtown Eastside of Vancouver and in several Canadian provinces, in big cities as well as in remote areas, thousands of girls and young women in Ciudad Juárez dead or disappeared after working in the *maquiladoras* along the American border, black American women who have died at the hands of police forces, as shown in the 2015 updated report "Say her name: Resisting police brutality against black women" (co-authored by Kimberlé Williams Crenshaw, who coined the notion of intersectionality). . . . So many dead women, serial murders committed by individuals often unidentified but whose actions are acknowledged by a society that gives itself permission to turn a blind eye to certain populations, and in doing so, silently banishes them.

This is the serialization of girls, the face of women as ornament, plastic, walking dead, a femininity reified and commodified, the right to act, in reality, on women's bodies as though they were property – pure objects, pure images.

Photo by Martine Delvaux and Éléonore Delvaux-Beaudoin

13

Mirror, Mirror

Girls wear a skin that isn't a skin, a skin we imagine to be a naked-ness, which, once we've seen it, makes us believe that we have at last gained access to knowledge. To see girls naked would mean seeing them for real, seeing real girls.

Even clothed, aren't serial girls always in fact the image of naked girls? As if, upon these girls who all look the same and all wear the same clothes (be it costumes or uniforms, as with the Tiller Girls and other dancing girls, or fashion designer collections), we superimpose a fanta-sized, imagined nudity, a nudity that, ultimately, is the *true* image, the one we look for and that we see beyond what is presented. The pleasure provided by the sight of serial girls has to do with their appearance, an apparition as affecting as that of nude bodies.

○ ○ ○

"*Men act* and *women appear*. Men look at women. Women watch them-selves being looked at." These are the now-famous words of John Berger in *Ways of Seeing*.[1] Men act, women appear. Men look, women are looked at. Moreover: women *watch themselves* being looked at; they look at their own image in the making. Surveyed and surveying, women seem to be a dual object of vision, a dual sight.

In 1972, Berger used images to reflect on sexual difference, proposing a feminist reading of our society where women, because they are always the object of men's gaze, because this is in a way their function, the place they occupy most, end up being split in two. According to Berger, women are looked at so much and in such a way that the image takes their place; it becomes impossible to distinguish the woman from the image. It could even be said that sometimes the image does such a good job of occupying a woman's place that a real woman would be willing to die in order to surrender to it, and be replaced by the artifice-image, the fash-ion-image, the skin-image that makes flesh obsolete.

Hence, Nelly Arcan: when she takes her life, is she not also putting the image to death? She is often accused of having dug her own grave, of having been caught in the trap of appearances (by choosing to transform her body through cosmetic surgery and entering the media-circus ring) and paying with her life. She is accused, as if women have a choice, as if they can go on strike against the image. Arcan is the target of these accusations because we prefer to ignore the implicit commentary that underlined her self-representation, the way she staged herself as an image in order to throw in our faces what is left of what society does to women. As we also fail to recognize Arcan's ownership of this, and her desire to play with the image (as shown by the photographs of herself she chose to stage).[2]

Nelly Arcan asks whether women can succeed in freeing themselves from image, and if they could, what would be left of them. Would there be anything underneath the image? Is it possible to live as a woman outside the image? Does everything begin at that moment when the girl appears, at the moment of the first image, the first capture, the first abduction? I'm thinking here about descriptions of childhood photographs by writers (Marguerite Duras and Annie Ernaux, for example), a scene also found in Nelly Arcan's posthumous text "La Robe" (The dress). This scene is the seed, with Nelly Arcan as with so many others, of an initial, original shame.

> So there I was, teetering on the rock. I was wearing jeans and a sky-blue T-shirt with a grinning Mickey Mouse decal. My sandy hair was cut short; it was the same as it is now, same colour, same length, the same counter-performance of a sandy blonde, lacking lustre. It's as if I've spent my whole life on that rock. My two hands were curiously behind my back, at butt height, as if I was trying to keep something from falling. I was holding something with my hands, something to do with my butt, when someone took a picture of me. . . . My face, frozen in panic, mouth opened in an "O," I didn't want the camera to take my picture but it triumphed over my refusal.[3]

The memory linked to that scene is imprinted with shame. It could be termed a *blushing* memory: had the little girl pooed in her panties? Was that what she was trying to hide? This is what she believed for years, until her mother told her, when she was an adult, that she was trying to hide a hole, "just a hole. . . ."

o o o

I wonder if each one of us does not have, in her memory, a photo of herself as a little girl, taken to make us blush. Photos to be ashamed of for a whole lifetime. Shameful photos taken against our will and exhibited on the walls of our parents' homes.

This I remember. It is a Sunday afternoon in the garden. My uncle is holding the camera, he directs it at me, sitting in the grass, head in hands, elbows resting on my knees, legs lifted up, slightly spread open. A sundress with a gathered bodice, as was the style then, white cotton panties slightly showing through. In the photo, I am furious. The uncle, an amateur photographer, wanted to capture a child's furious face and in order to do so, he had to trap her. She eventually let her picture be taken, and for years afterwards lived with the bitter memory of that moment, when she surrendered.

On that day, did I let go of my image? Was that the day I officially entered the image system, akin to debutante balls that enthrone young ladies, all alike in their white dresses, in the realm of a femininity that is fit to marry, buy, consume, and reproduce?

We tend to think that nakedness is not a concern for children. Children would appear not to know nakedness, not to realize that they are naked when they are. Yet on that day, even though I wasn't really naked because I was fully clothed, I experienced the sensation of nudity. In the shot that was taken, I was forced to recognize my image and, like Nelly Arcan's (female) narrator, I was instantly plunged into shame, "riveted to myself." As Emmanuel Levinas writes,

> Shame arises each time we are unable to make others forget [*faire oublier*] our basic nudity. It is related to everything we would like to hide and that we cannot bury or cover up. In shameful nakedness, what is thus in question is not only the body's nakedness. However, it is not by pure chance that, under the poignant form of modesty, shame is primarily connected to our body.[4]

Shame happens when we feel that we have been taken hostage by our own image, prison-image, corset-image, the image that "put me in my place." The worst sadism, here, lies in an image that eventually takes up the whole space, to the extent of suffocating the woman or girl who is its subject. Who is the *I* whom, when looking at the photo, I recognized and chose as my double – that image that compounds me, as Berger puts it, in the manner of serial girls hidden inside me like nesting dolls and that I am striving, here, to unwrap?

o o o

Animals also seem unaware of nakedness. Neither naked nor clothed, when we fit them with an article of clothing, they look ridiculous. Their skin *is* their coat, and it is hard to imagine an animal experiencing shame or shyness. Yet there is one image of animals, in my view, that must be taken into account within the context of serial girls: the image of animal carcasses hanging in a slaughterhouse. An image not unlike that of a RealDoll factory in California, where headless silicone bodies are suspended by hooks and metal chains to allow them to dry after being moulded.

In Rome's Testaccio neighbourhood, the old nineteenth-century *mattatoio* (slaughterhouse) has been transformed into a museum – the MACRO (Museum of Contemporary Art of Rome) Future – where fashion shows are sometimes held. The architects of the MACRO Future preserved much of the original buildings, considered the most important surviving example of Roman industrial architecture, as well as a number of instruments that were integrated into the museum's design – including the pens, bathtubs, and ceilings where carcasses were hung.

The link between feminism and animal rights is well known, ever since the suffragettes' opposition to vivisection: in the image of the Brown Dog tied up and dissected without anaesthesia, they recognized the image of suffragettes force-fed during a hunger strike, of a hysteric who was sterilized, of a woman lying with legs spread open on a gynecologist's table.... Current eco-feminists, such as Carol J. Adams, Josephine Donovan, and Lisa Kemmerer, spotlight the close connection between what is done to women and what is done to animals, the place they are assigned within our thought patterns. In *The Pornography of Meat*,[5] Carol J. Adams describes the binary organization in the following way. On the one hand, there is category "A," consisting of men, whites, culture, civilization, capital, human beings. On the other, there is category "non-A": women, nonwhites, nature, bodies, Aboriginal people, work, and, of course, nonhuman animals. The critique of binary thinking is at the core of feminism, be it from a materialist or a deconstructionist perspective, for in any case, this way of organizing thought is the cornerstone of women's oppression. Moreover, binary thinking is at the heart of oppression in general, which, in view of that, must be read from an intersectional viewpoint (that is, factoring in gender in addition to social class, ethnicity, sexual preference, and ultimately *species*) in order to be sensitive to how different forms of oppression intersect, play against each other in the intensification of multiple forms of power and of dominations.

According to this logic, women are animals like all others. Besides, we must recognize that not only the animals most consumed (chickens and their eggs, turkeys, cows as minced beef and their milk) but also those found at the core of the meat industry, used as reproduction machines, are female animals (sows, for example). Many researchers have documented the suffering endured by animal mothers when their offspring are taken away from them too soon (as is the case for cows separated from their calves, for example).[6]

o o o

As early as 1920, we see, in the words of Virginia Woolf, the birth of the equation between women and animals, an image of masculine domination in relation to animals. Here, birds are the focus of Woolf's argument, at a time when the "Plumage Bill" – aimed at ending, in England, the plucking of birds for decorative use (as with *aigrettes*, made of egret feathers) – was smothered. Woolf replies to a journalist who, in defence of the proposed bill and of birds, accuses women who purchase feathers of being insensitive to the fate of animals. If the bill is smothered, millions of birds are destined to die and, worse yet, to be tortured, writes Woolf. Of course this is true: women stop to admire displays of feathers. But if they do so, it is because "the plumes seem to be the natural adornment of spirited and fastidious life, the very symbol of pride and distinction,"[7] and because this marker is valorized by the society they live in. Indeed, they cannot do without this symbol.

In order for women of child-bearing age to wear such feathers, birds will have to be killed, and since the feathers are more beautiful during nesting time, their chicks will also be left to die. But who kills the birds? asks Woolf. It is men who carry out this task with their own hands, so that their wives may pin the long plumes onto their hats and look fashionable when seen on their husband's arm. It was also men who were called upon to vote on the "Plumage Bill," intended to end the exploitation of birds, which they refused to do (the quorum went unmet five times).

But in actual fact, Woolf concludes, this defence of birds, which she herself composed – is it not a commentary on the injustice done to women? Torturing birds in the name of women, doing to birds what is done to women, accusing women of being responsible for or insensitive to the fate of birds. . . . Such are the many strategies used to deny what Woolf and today's eco-feminists denounce: women are treated like animals, and if the mistreatment of animals continues, then there is no reason for the abuse of women to cease. As Carol J. Adams writes: "Recognizing harm to animals as interconnected to controlling behavior by violent men is one aspect of recognizing the interrelatedness of all violence in a gender hierarchical world."[8]

If Woolf is this concerned with bird feathers, it is because of an undeniable connection between the ornamental object (accessory, garment, beauty products) and the woman in society to whom makeup (made from animal products), furs, duvets, leather goods are sold. . . . Woolf notes how women are made into accomplices of animal abuse by the fact that the male gaze makes certain demands on their appearance. Of course, things have changed since 1920, and Woolf's argument could appear outdated. Yet her argument remains timely. In various ways and for all kinds of reasons, as well as in different contexts, women today still have to deal with a number of demands as to the way they present themselves, be it to attend British high society horse-racing events, to go out to a trendy New York bar, to go to work in a Montreal office tower or in a Paris boutique. . . . As regards the fashion industry, the family as institution, the workplace, sex and emotional life, health, and so on, women and animals (the consumption of animal flesh as food, as well as what covers animals' bodies, which we use to cover our own) remain connected.

○ ○ ○

Recall the now-classic photograph published by *Hustler* on its June 1978 cover. It shows a woman half-stuffed head first into a meat grinder with the following sentence as the main title: "We will no longer hang women up like pieces of meat. – Larry Flint." A fine example of newspeak, these words by *Hustler* founder and owner Flint suggest exactly the opposite of what they say: rather, women will be constantly exhibited as pieces of meat. But there is more. The way the image is presented highlights the model's legs: head and chest swallowed up by the meat grinder, only the long legs are left, not unlike the ones in the DIM pantyhose ads mentioned earlier, like the legs belonging to the Tiller Girls, the Rockettes, and other dancing girls. Shimmery, oiled, tanned, and well shaped, the woman's legs resemble chicken legs as much as they do dancers' legs.

Indeed, women *are* meat. Hunted, purchased, grilled. Everywhere, food, and especially meat, is compared to the female body, just like the vocabulary of food is used to represent woman – from "It's a grill!" (a culinary variation of "It's a girl," which began this essay) to "Fish and Chicks" by way of "The Men's Club. Where everything is mouthwatering, even the food!"[9]

In *Sister Species*, Karen Davis connects the dots between her youthful obsession with Hitler's concentration and extermination camps and her commitment to animal protection. Disturbed by concentration camp testimonies, she tells about putting herself *in the skin* of people forced to live in Nazi camps: "Inwardly, I was driven to 'go' to places where I imagined how it would be to no longer feel like, or be, oneself, though still remain alive and functioning."[10] Years later, as an activist and eco-feminist, she discerns her concern for animals in that early sensitivity to Nazi camp victims. And the question underlying her story (what does being oneself mean in such circumstances?) finds reinforcement in the one put forth by Primo Levi, mentioned at the beginning of this essay: "Consider if this is a man."[11]

o o o

In *Eternal Treblinka*, Charles Patterson attributes the following sentence to Theodor Adorno: "Auschwitz begins whenever someone looks at a slaughterhouse and thinks: they're only animals."[12] These words echo what Adorno says in Aphorism 68 of *Minima Moralia*:

> The ceaselessly recurrent expression that savages, blacks, Japanese resemble animals, or something like apes, already contains the key to the pogrom. The possibility of this latter is contained in the moment that a mortally wounded animal looks at a human being in the eye. The defiance with which they push away this gaze – "it's after all only an animal" – is repeated irresistibly in atrocities to human beings, in which the perpetrators must constantly reconfirm this "only an animal," because they never entirely believed it even with animals.[13]

In a similar manner, artist Judy Chicago, when she was studying the Holocaust, established a correlation between the commercial slaughter of animals and the industrialized carnage of humans. Feminist and activist Aviva Cantor writes that nowhere is patriarchy's iron grip more manifest than in animal oppression, which serves as template for other forms of oppression.

> What made the Holocaust possible (and some may argue inevitable) is the fact of patriarchy, and the fact that patriarchal values dominate our society. . . . Men seek power over each other, over women, over children, over animals, over the natural world, and justify this on grounds of utility. It is these values which have made the Holocaust possible.[14]

Finally, in *Eternal Treblinka*, Charles Patterson spotlights both the relationship to food, and more specifically to meat, maintained by the SS running death camps,[15] and the fact that a number of executioners inside the camps came from animal farming and food industry backgrounds: dairy farms, slaughterhouses, butcher shops. . . .

This connection is not mere anecdote; it is a fundamental link. Rereading the Nazi regime through the lens of the treatment of animals, Patterson exposes the close tie between industrial slaughter and human extermination. Terming humans "animals" is an important sign, he writes, insofar as it sets the scene for humiliation, exploitation, and murder.[16] He gives the example of Turks identifying Armenians as livestock during the years leading to the genocide, just like the Nazis called Jews "rats," and how Hutus called Tutsis "insects." In *Mein Kampf*, Hitler said that Jews carried germs, contaminated art and culture, infiltrated the economy, and poisoned racial health.[17]

Thus, it is not an innocent fact that at Ravensbrück, a concentration camp for women, the Germans gave the name "Lapins Project" to the medical experiments carried out on the inmates there and, of course, nicknamed them "rabbit girls."[18]

Playboy Bunnies at the Playboy Mansion, Los Angeles, CA, on July 23, 2011, © Glenn Francis,
www.PacificProDigital.com

14

Bunnies

W hen I was little I had pet rabbits. We lived in the country and, to make me happy, my parents bought me both a male and a female from a nearby breeder. At night, we often heard the cages, set up in the garden under my bedroom window, rattling against the wall of the house. Soon a litter of bunnies was born. Months passed, and the rabbit family kept growing, until one night, in the dark, some men came to get them. They took all of them, except for two of the first-born. The fully grown baby rabbits were to be slaughtered. One night, they would be served to me on a plate, and I would refuse to eat them.

The day after the night the rabbits were taken, I went to feed the remaining ones and discovered, at the bottom of the cage, a pile of dead bunnies, a mass of indiscernible pink flesh except for their tiny faces with eyes shut tight. I didn't know whether one of the females had given birth in the general panic, or if the young were already born when the men came and had not been seen in the darkness, or if the men had seen them but, as baby rabbits are not edible, had left them to die.

I was devastated and horrified. I don't know what connection I made between dead baby rabbits and my own body that day; I only know that they have never stopped haunting me. I tell myself that they are a part of who I am today.

o o o

In *Les mots et les femmes* (Words and women), Marina Yaguello proposes a list of terms used to depreciate women. As a pioneer in the reading of language as a depository and vehicle of misogyny, she lists the thousand and one ways of naming women to make them feel inferior. Be they insults directed at women or feminized words used to insult men, the feminine is, in every case, the tool of a devaluation. While certain things may have changed since the publication of her essay in 1978, the linguistic subordination of women remains and is exerted through, among other things, the lexical field concerning animals. The poultry theme underscored by Yaguello remains central (*poule, poulette, cocotte, pintade*: chicken, chick, tart, pet or sweetie) and goes on to *truie, vache, biche, chatte* (sow, cow, doe or darling, pussy), and finally *chienne* – whose English equivalent, *bitch,* has been reclaimed by a feminist discourse, as seen in the eponymous *Bitch* magazine, and the current trend among young women who call each other *bitch* as an equivalent of *sisters* or *girls.*

As Simone de Beauvoir wrote in *The Second Sex*:

> The word "female" evokes a saraband of images . . . monstrous and stuffed, the queen termite reigning over the servile males; the praying mantis and the spider, gorged on love, crushing their partners and gobbling them up; the dog in heat running through back alleys . . . the monkey showing herself off brazenly, sneaking away with flirtatious hypocrisy. . . . Man projects all females at once onto woman.[1]

More recently, Irene Lopez Rodriguez has shown that the animal metaphors adopted to designate women, though diverse, tend to link them to small, domesticated animals.[2] These terms have negative connotations. Female animals are subordinated, or, if they are in a position of power, figured as threatening, while male animals represent desiring, positively connotated subjects. Women are burdened with the names of animals whose lesser value is due to their availability. Accordingly, domesticated animals signal a close proximity through the life we share; farm animals, a lesser proximity because they are almost domesticated and we can eat them; game animals, a certain distance but accessible (these animals are wild but nonetheless edible because they can be caught); and wild animals, at a total distance because they escape humans and are not edible. In this context, it is the *female rabbit* that holds my attention: as in, *She breeds like a rabbit. . . .*

In linguistic dissymmetry as we know it, a *chaud lapin* (stud) is seen as laudable, admirable even (with the added value of being seen as a great seducer), while a woman who breeds like a rabbit (*lapine*) is devalued: the "sexual" woman is at once belittled, and when this is done verbally, it is through a sexual reference, image, or undertone. The female rabbit, therefore, produces the image of a sexual girl merged with a state approaching abnormality (producing a lot of children and *too* easily; making love *too much* and *too often*), which refers back to animality.

As an animal, the rabbit is interesting due to the place it occupies: it is a small farm animal that can be both domesticated *and* eaten, appreciated for its fur and for its meat. On the edge of wildness. It frequents humans (despite the limits of possible interactions), whose prey it is as well. And it is here, on this threshold, that women are found.

The female rabbit (*lapine*), therefore, because it belongs to the farming world as well as the familial, stuffed animals and children's stories.

The female rabbit, also, because it is the image of an animal popularized by *Playboy* that has become the major sexual symbol as it relates to this warren that represents women.

o o o

Recall that in 1968, four hundred feminists demonstrated against the Miss America beauty pageant being held in Atlantic City. The event is imprinted in our memory as the one where women burned their bras.[3] Unfurling a large banner reading "Women's Liberation," they captured worldwide attention through their goal of denouncing the ideal feminine being crowned by beauty contests. In the manifesto written on the occasion (an important document in regards to second-wave feminism), *Playboy* is mentioned among the ten ways of objectifying women:

1. The Degrading Mindless-Boob-Girlie Symbol. The Pageant contestants epitomize the roles we are all forced to play as women. The parade down the runway blares the metaphor of the 4-H Club county fair, where the nervous animals are judged for teeth, fleece, etc., and where the best "Specimen" gets the blue ribbon. So are women in our society forced daily to compete for male approval, enslaved by ludicrous "beauty" standards we ourselves are conditioned to take seriously.

2. Racism with Roses. Since its inception in 1921, the Pageant has not had one Black finalist, and this has not been for a lack of test-case contestants. There has never been a Puerto Rican, Alaskan, Hawaiian, or Mexican-American winner. Nor has there ever been a true Miss America – an American Indian.

3. Miss America as Military Death Mascot. The highlight of her reign each year is a cheerleader-tour of American troops abroad – last year she went to Vietnam to pep-talk our husbands, fathers, sons and boyfriends into dying and killing with a better spirit. She personifies the "unstained patriotic American womanhood our boys are fighting for." The Living Bra and the Dead Soldier. We refuse to be used as Mascots for Murder.

4. The Consumer Con-Game. Miss America is a walking commercial for the Pageant's sponsors. Wind her up and she plugs your prod-

uct on promotion tours and TV – all in an "honest, objective"
endorsement. What a shill.

5. Competition Rigged and Unrigged. We deplore the encourage-
ment of an American myth that oppresses men as well as women:
the win-or-you're-worthless competitive disease. The "beauty
contest" creates only one winner to be "used" and forty-nine
losers who are "useless."

6. The Woman as Pop Culture Obsolescent Theme. Spindle, muti-
late, and then discard tomorrow. What is so ignored as last year's
Miss America? This only reflects the gospel of our Society, according to Saint Male: women must be young, juicy, malleable – hence
age discrimination and the cult of youth. And we women are
brainwashed into believing this ourselves!

7. The Unbeatable Madonna-Whore Combination. Miss America
and Playboy's centerfold are sisters over the skin. To win
approval, we must be both sexy and wholesome, delicate but able
to cope, demure yet titillatingly bitchy. Deviation of any sort
brings, we are told, disaster: "You won't get a man!!"

8. The Irrelevant Crown on the Throne of Mediocrity. Miss America
represents what women are supposed to be: inoffensive, bland,
apolitical. If you are tall, short, over or under what weight The
Man prescribes you should be, forget it. Personality, articulate-
ness, intelligence, and commitment – unwise. Conformity is the
key to the crown – and, by extension, to success in our Society.

9. Miss America as Dream Equivalent To – In this reputedly democratic society, where every little boy supposedly can grow up to be
President, what can every little girl hope to grow to be? Miss
America. That's where it's at. Real power to control our own lives
is restricted to men, while women get patronizing pseudo-power,
an ermine clock and a bunch of flowers; men are judged by their
actions, women by appearance.

10. Miss America as Big Sister Watching You. The pageant exercises
Thought Control, attempts to sear the Image onto our minds, to
further make women oppressed and men oppressors; to enslave
us all the more in high-heeled, low-status roles; to inculcate false
values in young girls; women as beasts of buying; to seduce us to
our selves before our own oppression.

Miss America and her many avatars have survived and even produced
offspring, as seen on the reality TV show *Toddlers and Tiaras* (airing from
2008 to 2013), which followed little girls and their parents involved in the

beauty pageant industry. There was also the murder of young JonBenét Ramsey in 1996, a crime that lifted the veil of that pedophilia-tinged world where little girls are dressed and made up like adult women, and parade in front of an audience in a way that is at best worrisome.

o o o

The feminists of 1968 not only set fire to their bras; they also threw away pots and pans, false eyelashes, high heels, cosmetics, curling irons, and issues of *Playboy*, perceived as the principal agent of cultural pimping, into a giant Freedom Trash Can. Ultimately, what they sought to eliminate was women's becoming-ornament, those thousands of ways to kill a woman by "plastifying" her.

In January 1963, a young Gloria Steinem, a journalist (before she became the famous feminist), is hired as a Bunny by the New York Playboy Club. She is twenty-eight years old, four years over the age limit set by the business; she has chosen a pseudonym that is ordinary enough not to arouse any suspicion and has successfully completed her mission, wearing a high-cut satin bodysuit, a cotton tail, and rabbit ears. Five months later, she published "A Bunny's Tale," an account of her experience, in *Show* magazine, a publication that helped build the feminist movement.

Steinem's article appeared the same year as Betty Friedan's essay *The Feminine Mystique* and Sylvia Plath's novel *The Bell Jar*, less than one year after Marilyn Monroe's death, and just as Playboy Clubs, and therefore Bunnies, too, were proliferating across the US. Hugh Hefner's mission was to sexually liberate men and women, all the while keeping the latter in their place – sassy and shameless, free and available for sexual encounters without matrimonial commitment while remaining submissive. Having scripted them into the never-ending cat-and-mouse seduction games typical of exchanges between men and women, *Playboy* incited men to see the girls as not so much liberated but accessible, sexually attractive creatures to be bedded and consumed "serially." As one of the captions in the *Playboy* colouring book asserts: "It does not matter which is which. The girls' haircolors are interchangeable. So are the girls."[4] Playmates, like Bunnies, are essentially all the same: white, tall, blond, and curvy.[5] The pictures of Hugh Hefner surrounded by girls who live with him in his mansion, be they "official" companions or various Playmates, perfectly illustrate this creation of the *Playboy* world, founded on Hefner-the-god flanked by a panoply of blond nymphettes.

Paradoxically, the success of *Playboy*, that peculiar planet-of-women, is not unrelated to the fear of a "woman-centered society."[6] In the early sixties, and facing the rising feminist movement, Hefner categorically opposes women's influence and its castrating effect on cultural productions. Hence his slogan: "We think it's a man's world, or it should be."[7] According to Hefner, woman was made to complete man, first by fully participating in sexual life (as the perfect erotic partner) and then by staying in her place by occupying jobs other than those traditionally done by men to avoid robbing them of their prestige.[8] In actual fact, the ideal Playmate was pure surface, a perfect image of pleasure and leisure. She was the "New Girl," a young "post-feminist" (if we are to believe Hefner's word) venturing into a life of sexual freedom and drugs, diving naked into pleasure and the politics of "Bobby Kennedy and Bobby Dylan, the New Left and Civil Rights."[9] Against bra-wearing and pro-abortion, *Playboy*'s position was a veritable double-edged sword, setting a trap of apparent feminist liberation while actually seeking to maintain the status quo.

That is the manipulative paradox Gloria Steinem exposed in her article. She does not believe Hugh Hefner for one second when he claims that the essays published in his magazine proclaim the emancipation of the sexual revolution. She accesses the inner circle of Bunnies to reveal its underpinnings, and this starts as soon as she reaches the doors of the Club: "Here Bunny, Bunny, Bunny!" yells a guard to direct her toward the interview room.

It was only after receiving the Bunny Manual, meeting the Bunny Mother, and attending slide-show lessons dispensed by the Bunny Father, after being made to try on an undersized, corset-like bunny suit whose bosom must be stuffed with cotton, and after undergoing a gynecological examination (with blood test and swab to detect any STD), that Steinem officially became a Playboy Bunny: "Bunnies are not born; bunnies are made. And they are made with the help of a whole army of people."[10]

Poorly paid (contrary to what *Playboy* posted as a promise in its job offers in the newspapers), forced to work long hours without a break and under constant surveillance (demerit points for lateness or non-conforming physical appearance; presence of a private detective hired to expose any girls liable to engage in prostitution with clients), there is nothing enviable about the Bunny's life, writes Steinem. So while girls are forbidden to keep company with clients, this same behaviour is allowed when it comes to VIPs (Very Important Playboys) who own a special "key." Hefner speaks a language that says the opposite of reality: "We naturally do not tolerate any merchandising of the Bunnies."[11] And yet the use of the plural ("Bunnies" as a class) clearly expresses this commodification of the girls, as does the use of the generic as proper name: as with nuns who are called Sister X, Bunnies see their given names come in second (Bunny Marie, Bunny Gloria . . .), *Playboy* thus becoming their family or their religion. With shades of *1984*, immersed in diffuse surveillance, secrets, and restrictions ("Nobody around here ever tells us anything," confides one of them[12]), Bunnies have more in common with toy animals and showgirls than with modern women: "There are times when a woman reading *Playboy* feels a little like a Jew reading a Nazi manual,"[13] says Steinem to Hefner during an interview for *McCall's Magazine* in 1970. Constantly harassed by clients and watched by Bunny Mothers, Playboy Club serial girls are in reality child-women, borrowing from Lolita as much as from dolls and mannequins.

Is there such a huge difference between the Playboy Club and the ordinary world? As Gloria Steinem came to conclude, after her stint at the Playboy Club: "All women are Bunnies."[14]

o o o

Even the architecture of the New York Playboy Club contributed to the confusion between woman and object. Behind the huge glass wall fronting the entire building, "all of us," wrote Steinem, "customers and Bunnies alike, were a living window display."[15] But there is more: as Beatriz Preciado shows in *Pornotopia*, the *Playboy* logic is profoundly masculinist, committed at the same time to both a relationship with architecture (particularly the bachelor pad that is the Playboy penthouse) and its use of serial girls. For if the reader is invited to follow the example of the "indoorsman" promoted by *Playboy*, a man wearing slippers and a satin dressing gown who cohabitates with a bevy of blonds like so many little girls or dolls,[16] he is only to make himself the centre of his own universe. In his masculinist revisiting of a room of one's own, Hefner encourages men's reappropriation of the domestic space, which indeed belongs to them also, and is "radically unlike the 'habitat' of the American nuclear family."[17]

Contrary to the 1950s' new single-family suburban home, where women labour as "unpaid full-time domestic and sexual workers, for the benefit of consumption and (re)production,"[18] the playboy finds freedom in his penthouse apartment, and in the bedroom, "a party room."[19] In this new relationship to domestic space (strongly promoted by Hefner through, among other means, articles on architecture and interior design), the man finds himself "on the threshold of femininity"[20] – hence the importance of his association with groups of naked girls: heterosexual eroticism guaranteeing that this is neither a women's nor a gay magazine.

In this "Adult Disneyland," as Hefner calls it, man is no longer the soldier he was at the onset of the Second World War. He has become a kind of James Bond, "impenetrable, dual, seductive, chameleonic, and sophisticated,"[21] a consumer of Bond girls who are all identical yet different, like in a doll collection. Between the sexual morals of suburban life and the feminist revolution, this is the bachelor Hugh Hefner invented, the ultimate Ken with Big Brother ways, surveying – unknown to the girls – a collection of undressed Barbies: *Playmates*, the *girls next door*.

○ ○ ○

The playboy's success, explains Preciado, depended on the exclusion of the three traditional feminine figures: mother, spouse, and mistress. The bachelor pad, where the man lives alone, comes with multiple conquests, a flock of more or less anonymous feminine faces. The Playmate photographed in the pages of the magazine corresponds to this new feminine figure, a mate to play with, as the term makes clear. If, like fashion models scouted in the streets, the Playmate belongs to the ordinary world ("Potential playmates are all around you,"[22] it used to say in *Playboy* magazine), she lives in the pages of the magazine, and more specifically in the centrefold.[23]

Playboy is said to have contributed to a liberalization of sexual mores, in the wake of the Kinsey Reports, of the contraceptive pill and the decriminalization of abortion, opposing American puritanism and promoting a free sex life made possible for ordinary folk – the Playmate intended to be seen as the embodiment of a sexual all-American girl. In fact, like Eve alongside Adam, Playboy Bunnies appeared after the invention of the *chaud lapin* (stud) bachelor, who was Hefner's target reader. And according to some, they embodied something akin to rebels as regards traditional femininity.

But beyond this sexual liberation there remains an image-woman, serial girls who are first and foremost ornamental. Their primary function is to serve masturbation, a hand gesture that is the same as page-turning, as Preciado so astutely suggests.

○ ○ ○

There is an obvious link between the Playboy Bunny and the Rabbit vibrator that the character Charlotte is unable to separate herself from in a famous episode of *Sex and the City*. As free as they seem to be to frolic through fields of sex, Bunnies are nevertheless under the controlling gaze of warren-master Hefner – while Charlotte, obsessed with her pink vibrator equipped with rabbit ears that perhaps provides her with more pleasure than any human male sex organ ever had ("I'd just rather stay home with the Rabbit than go out with men!"), involves her own body in a languorous and seemingly endless masturbation session.

At the time of first writing this book, the hit cult series *Sex and the City* had just turned fifteen. As journalist Nathalie Collard asks:

> Was *Sex and the City* a feminist series? Without a doubt. In its own way – and a little in Madonna's way – it introduced us to financially self-sufficient women who enjoyed seducing and owned their sexuality. In other words, the four friends in *Sex and the City* were women who took charge of their lives but often paid a price for their autonomy and independence. The kind of character not seen on TV since *Maude* (played by the wonderful Bea Arthur) and Mary Tyler Moore.[24]

Of course, *Sex and the City*'s feminist discourse is far from being simple and universally approved of (I will get back to this). Nevertheless, Charlotte's marriage to her Rabbit is part of an all-powerful autonomy that goes back to pro-sex and queer feminism. Pioneers Annie Sprinkle, Nina Hartley, and Candida Royalle, feminist versions of Hugh Hefner, reclaim in their own way the means of pornography for purposes of sexual education and specifically pro-woman pleasure, casting aside imposed, confiscated, policed, normalized sexuality.[25]

○ ○ ○

"The difference between pornography and erotica is lighting." These words from pro-pornography feminist Gloria Leonard have become legend. They are even quoted by B. Ruby Rich in Virginie Despentes' 2009 documentary *Mutantes* (Mutants). It is the witticism used to silence those who continue to believe in a basic, formal difference between pornography and eroticism, between sex scenes deemed vulgar and others that would appear to display good taste. A belief akin to a familiar stance on the part of intellectuals, as Linda Williams reminds us, who generally refuse to acknowledge that pornography excites them – preferring instead to say that it bores them. As though one could not find it exciting *and* maintain a critical eye and aesthetic standards.

The problem posed by porn, writes Virginie Despentes in *King Kong Theory*, "is first and foremost that it hits the blind corner of reason. . . . The hard-on or wetness comes first; wondering why follows on behind. . . . Porn images don't give us any choice."[26] Porn talks to us directly about our own desires. And the pornographic imagination is anything but ordinary, as Susan Sontag noted in 1970. There is nothing ordinary about being moved by a sexually explicit image or sentence. It is not something to be dismissed out of hand. Instead, it should be examined, just like any other form of knowledge. And this is what pro-sex feminists do. They refuse to turn their backs on pornography and instead approach it head on. They analyze it, get involved with it, reinvent it, produce it, and thus move beyond the porn industry, whose effect is not only the production of normed sexuality but also the big-screen display (and in many cases in inhumanely deplorable circumstances) of serial girls.

In *Mutantes*, Despentes interviews women who assert that they chose to work in the porn industry. Their approach is more or less the following: they want to be in the driver's seat of sexual representation and no longer its victims mowed down on the sidewalk. By accepting to satisfy their own fantasies, whatever they may be (and taking charge of film production), they are making a feminist gesture. For them, the word *porn*, once diverted from its offensive content, has the potential to become a site of identity construction. Porn, with such a negative reputation, becomes a space that is a bit clearer in the words and in the eyes of these women. And in the case of lesbian pornography, we could say that love between women is hidden sexuality – save for the version offered up for heterosexual benefit – that this invisibility is recovered, revisited in certain cultural objects such as the TV series *The L Word*[27] (a gay version of *Sex and the City*, some say with irony: "Same sex, different city"), which produces something different under the guise of just "giving male viewers what they want."

In *The L Word*, the spotlighting of sex between women operates on two fronts: first, what is seen resembles what we have already seen (the fully lit staging of sex conforming to what heterosexual movies and television produce); second, what is seen escapes us, plays with shadows and nuances, and is akin to a flickering, uncertain light that endlessly calls for another desire (the sexuality between women represented here nonetheless remains unique, the heterosexual bait proving insufficient, in my view, to remove this uniqueness).

The question of light recalls the image Virginie Despentes gives, in an interview, of the love life she now leads outside heterosexuality:

> The possibility of being out, it was like a liberation . . . but, you know, unexpected, like Bruce Willis when he's cornered on the subway in flames, he sees an exit far off in the distance, I really felt like that, then suddenly, a light came on, because I was in such a bad way, I didn't feel at all comfortable with having the identity of a "35-year-old het- ero girl," the future didn't seem bright.[28]

For Despentes, this light at the end of the tunnel travels through the "important front for feminist resistance" that is pornography. Hence the importance of the *Baise-moi Girls* (Fuck-me girls), who inhabit sexuality, circulate inside it like territory to be conquered, a city in which to take to the streets and go forward, imprinting it with their presence.[29]

This is how Playboy Bunnies reinvent themselves, behind or in front of the camera, as true streetwalkers.[30]

Marilyn partículas de luz, by Miguel Ángel Coronel, 2012

15

Blonds

Moviegoers are unlikely to have forgotten Adrian Lyne's 1987 feature film *Fatal Attraction* – on one hand because of its sex scenes and the female character Alex's voracious appetite; on the other for the scene known as the "bunny boiler" (a pet rabbit plunged into a pot of boiling water). Starting from the bunny boiler, Lyne's film must be read backwards. That white rabbit, which the jilted mistress kills out of revenge, brings to light the film's use of colours, encoding them with certain values.

From the outset, the dark-haired father, mother, and child appear onscreen dressed in white. In a pristine setting, nuclear-family domesticity is represented as pure perfection, whiter than white. In contrast, Glenn Close's character, Alex, the future one-night stand of Michael Douglas's character Dan, and who eventually disrupts the family's life, wears a black dress and smoky eye makeup, this look styled to intensify her very blond head of hair. Later on, the camera takes us to Alex's loft, an industrial apartment located in New York's Meatpacking District. After this scene, whenever we see Alex (a sexual predator with an androgynous name) entering or leaving her loft, her body merges with those of men transporting carcasses of animals to be butchered. Though Alex's loft is a perfectly white space – walls, furniture, bedding, accessories – in contrast to Dan's colourful and messy family home, this whiteness turns out to be a trap: the femme fatale's lair. Indeed, the fatal attraction could be said to occur not between the characters played by Douglas and Close, but between their worlds, domestic and then suburban for the former, "bachelor pad" and urban for the latter. Finally, it is the rabbit incident that turns attraction into repulsion, as the mistress is driven to attacking the very emblem of ordinary, innocent domesticity: the white rabbit.

My detour through this film intends to establish a bridge between blonds and white rabbits. Like Alex in *Fatal Attraction*, whose white loft and blond hair might, through a condensation of images, bring to mind Marilyn Monroe, standing over a subway grate with her white halter dress flying up, this animal is eminently attractive because harmlessly, yet disturbingly, under the fluff hides unbridled sexual activity and the risk of being swallowed. The rabbit is halfway between the wild and the domesticated, at once animality, innocence, sex, and femininity. As for the blond, femme-child fatale, pure and hypersexualized, familiar and dangerous, she belongs to the same species.

○ ○ ○

Everybody knows gentlemen prefer blonds, and diamonds are a girl's best friend. Through some barbaric mathematical operation, we could conclude that, basically, blonds are diamond-girls whose radiant hair turns heads.

It is also well known that blondness is politically charged. It is a symbol of the Aryan race (Himmler claimed that if Nazi laws were strictly applied, the German people could be genetically transformed into a pure blond race within 120 years); the desire for blondness served as an argument for the extermination of Jews, said to be parasites (hair colour being part of the reason for their segregation), as well as for the development of the *Lebensborn* program. This was a two-part program: the first was the kidnapping of blond children for the purposes of Germanization; in the other, men and women who were deemed acceptable based on their racial and physical features were called upon to "make a child for Hitler."[1] Hitler himself, though dark-haired, was represented as a blond in words and in paintings. Actually, only Reinhard Heydrich, the outstandingly cruel "blond beast," chief of the Reich Main Security Office, corresponded to the Aryan ideal.

The blond ideal was prevalent in Stalin's Russia as well, serving to promote national unity in a huge country composed of diverse populations, many of them deported between 1930 and 1940 in order to invent "the great Russian people," young, vigorous, and blond with fair skin and blue eyes. And we find it in the same period under Roosevelt in the United States. There as well, blondness is at the heart of the illusion-making machine aimed at demonstrating American superiority, blond (racial) superiority winning against the dark beast: King Kong (1933) holds Fay Wray in his grip atop the Empire State Building. One year later, puritanism prevails with the introduction of the Production Code Administration and its censorship of Hollywood films. Sultry blonds reinvent themselves, go from vamp to voluptuous but become ingénues, pin-ups intended to boost the morale of the troops, their images sent to GIs stationed abroad.

o o o

But among blonds such as Venus, Elizabeth I (who was naturally red-haired but wore blond wigs), Grace Kelly, Jean Harlow, Lana Turner, Marlene Dietrich, Veronica Lake, Brigitte Bardot, Dalida, Anita Ekberg, Doris Day, Betty Grable, Princess Di, Farrah Fawcett, Pamela Anderson, Madonna, Scarlett Johansson, Lady Gaga . . . among all those blonds ranging from blond star to democratized blond next door,[2] Marilyn Monroe stands out as the quintessential blond. She died a year before the publication of Gloria Steinem's essay on Playboy Bunnies, and it was a nude photo of her, taken by photographer Tom Kelley for the 1949 calendar, that allowed the first issue of the magazine to sell 54,000 copies. Even though she hadn't yet become the platinum-blond Marilyn Monroe, she was already a blond; she was *the* blond, the first and the last, "after whom all blondes produced nothing but duplicates (as Warhol had anticipated), and the actress who constructed her blondness, inextricably, as her tomb."[3]

Andy Warhol, a blond himself (and quasi–alter ego of Marilyn Monroe, as suggested by photographer Christopher Makos's *Andy Warhol, Altered Image*, 1981), revealed the star's truth through his portraits: she was, in and of herself, already a whole series. The star was a cluster of not only reincarnations – characters, photos, paintings, parodies, pastiches – but also narratives, personal accounts, recollections, rumours, fantasies;[4] she became a brand, a line of mass-produced collectibles. As Arthur Miller wrote, her life and her death were born of the merging of individual pain with the insatiable appetite of a consumer culture. David Lynch's 2001 film *Mulholland Drive* deals with this as well; in Naomi Watts's traits we see Marilyn Monroe reappear, and also, depending on the camera angles, Meg Ryan, Cameron Diaz, Madonna . . . today's blonds.

Over time, as representations multiplied, Marilyn Monroe was made increasingly invisible. As she was destined to disappear for the benefit of an image larger than her own, we still strive – through publications and celebrations – to try to know who Marilyn was. Like the character Kitty in her ex-husband Arthur Miller's last play (*Finishing the Picture*, 2004), Marilyn Monroe was a face everybody talked about, fabricated by other people's words grafted to her skin, pigments and pixels that manufacture her identity by multiplying her ad infinitum, including fragments and drawings made of her hand and published as if to put flesh back onto a skeleton we ourselves had stripped.

From now on, Marilyn Monroe lives everywhere, and dies everywhere, at every moment. The second we think we've got her, she slips away. Transformed into pure ornament, over time she has become ghostly, airborne. And there is nothing to be done about it; it is too late to bring her back to Earth, to bring her back to life.

○ ○ ○

Quebec writer Nelly Arcan, her body handed over to silicone and scalpels, perpetually on display, extracted herself from the extreme commodification of which Marilyn was the object. Nelly Arcan, whose photos are often remakes of and direct references to famous images of Hollywood stars.[5] Nelly Arcan, whore, hysteric, and suicide victim, authored texts comparable to fables and fairy tales that leave us feeling like we have nothing to say because everything is provided at the outset, the story and its moral. What is Arcan saying if not something like: "Women are victims of the image imposed on them and that they are made to desire. Women are the object of a transaction they themselves are part of. Women are stuck in an endless Stockholm Syndrome. See, I am living proof of it. This is about my body. Even literature can't protect me."

Nelly Arcan existed in reality, and she died in reality, despite the fact that she had become an image. Like the women she portrayed, Nelly Arcan was an icon, the shooting star in our literary sky, little blond sister of Marilyn Monroe, to whom she was often compared. Nelly Arcan, like the sex-symbol actress she described in a review of Michel Schneider's book *Marilyn's Last Sessions* in 2006:

> For me, this woman has always been the sublime creature in extremely famous photos that were self-contained, playful, naughty, framing enticing poses; a highly sensual woman but also unsteady actress, radiant and insignificant, dead of an ambiguous overdose that was either accidental or organized, it has never been determined.[6]

She had never paid attention to this woman because "you don't read about legends you meet on a daily basis on posters. You don't read about what everyone talks about."[7]

Like many teenage girls, I loved Marilyn Monroe with a passion. I covered my bedroom walls with her face, collected photo albums and calendars, devoured books about the mysterious circumstances surrounding her death. My fascination fed on distance, on the fact that Marilyn and her story could only escape me. Just like we were fascinated by Nelly Arcan. We were fascinated by her, but did we read her? Did we read about her, and can we now write about her? It is by reading Nelly Arcan reading Michel Schneider reading Marilyn Monroe that I felt the desire to write about Nelly Arcan, and to reread her, and that I ask myself the question that has never stopped being asked concerning the last moments of the movie star's life: Who killed Nelly Arcan?

o o o

Nelly Arcan's image dazzled me as much as it worried me. Because she was brilliant. She haunted me when she was alive, and continues to haunt me now that she is dead. We went to the same cafés. We walked along the same streets. I ran into her in Saint-Louis Square, on Saint-Denis Street, near the restaurants on Prince-Arthur Street, in Montreal's Portuguese neighbourhood. She is gone and I still turn around to look at the platinum hair of girls I see on the street. I scrutinize their faces for a moment before remembering that it cannot be her, because Nelly Arcan is no longer with us. This is something I know; I did not believe it when it happened, and then I read her, and reread her, reread everything in order to write about her, once again fascinated, like astronomers who swear only by the stars tracked in the blueness of the sky. Nelly Arcan was our literary star.

When I saw Isabelle Fortier before she became Nelly Arcan, her hair was brown, and I stayed with the image of Nelly Arcan as a brunette. I loved that image just like I love the one of Norma Jean Baker, her long brown curls making her eyes seem lighter, her girl-next-door look on the first calendars she sold before becoming Marilyn Monroe, MM, the name she had chosen along with the blondness that allowed her to resemble other movie-screen blonds, in order "to not be a woman with reddish-brown hair,"[8] "Marilyn Monroe, Blonde, 37–23–36,"[9] as her imagined epitaph read. Marilyn refused to accept the presence of any other blond on a film set while she was there: "No other blondes. I'm the only blonde."[10] And to Truman Capote, who once told her that he thought she was a 100 percent real blond, she replied: "I am. But nobody's that natural. And, incidentally, fuck you."[11] Michel Schneider compares his novel to Marilyn's curls – it is "really false."[12] Marilyn Monroe exists in its pages like she existed on the screen: as an image. And this image is neither truer nor falser than she was. As she used to say: "Who does he think I am? Marilyn Monroe or something?"[13]

o o o

Girls are brunettes before they are stars. Blondness is what confirms
their star status in the cultural universe. Nelly Arcan became a blond as
soon as she became a writer. She became a blond writer, and when I
think about the Marilyn Monroe fragments published in 2012, I think
about Nelly Arcan, too. Nelly Arcan became blond because men prefer
blonds, and fairy tales, and Mattel, and Nazis, too. It is said that deep
down, even Cleopatra was a blond. Nelly Arcan was blond like the girls
she describes in her novel *Hysteric*, whose "pale skin was like a beacon in
the dark atmosphere of the bar,"[14] girls who "didn't need to move to be
noticed,"[15] girls we see, quite simply, and who turn the bar into a starry
sky. Nelly Arcan was one of them, but she had shone more brightly than
the others. It was impossible not to see her. Through her, literature had,
like Hollywood, found its very own blond. Nelly Arcan was literature's
whore (*fille publique*). It was easy; there was no shame in consuming her,
since she offered herself up as fodder. French writer Marguerite Duras
had done so before her. The whore from the Normandy coast had also
been literature's courtesan, even at seventy years old, with her uniform,
her rings, her lovers, her red wine, her ill temper, Duras, who everywhere
in her work depicted women who were sold, bartered, Duras, who put
writing on public display in the same way she recounted having given
herself to a Chinese lover long ago. The same can be said of Nelly Arcan.
After thousands of men in her bed, in her mouth, she lay down on the
page to be taken anew. How can we not feel uneasy about consuming
this girl's work, when her writing was like she was burning herself at the
stake? Nelly Arcan, like Huguette Gaulin and the everyday trend toward
"mythicizing necrophilia."[16]

Nelly Arcan is Michel Schneider's Marilyn Monroe: a goddess both
alive and dead. Nelly Arcan is Sylvia Plath, one of those hyper-gifted literary blonds who bleached her hair platinum after a suicide attempt and
before undertaking advanced studies at Oxford. It was after going blond
that she became a poet. It was said of Plath that she did not know what
she wanted: to embody the *all-American girl*,[17] the *feminine mystique*,[18]
or the rebel artist. She wound up being all those at once, at the cost of
her life. Perhaps Nelly Arcan also wanted to be everything at once, the
intellectual and the platinum blond, high class and trash. She wanted
the baby and the bathwater, and was bitterly resented for playing it that
way. People wanted her to choose. To settle, to appear or disappear once
and for all. Mostly she was resented for holding a mirror up to the face of

literature. For telling literature (for making it own up to the fact) that it too craves stars, blonds, even though it resents wanting them. Because deep down, literature feels slightly ashamed of operating in such a manner . . . of admitting that the literary universe is not so different from the set of a television show – cheap, profit-oriented, greedy, voyeuristic. And Nelly Arcan set the trap it fell into. Is that who Nelly Arcan was talking to? Was literature like the clients who dropped in on her Doctor Penfield Avenue address to enjoy her company?

o o o

With *Whore*, Nelly Arcan became everybody's blond, the one everybody desired and wanted to take, a blond with skin so fair it was translucent, a blond so blond she was obscure, so visible you could no longer see her. Nelly Arcan was so dazzling you could not look at her, like when children are forbidden to look at the sun, or at an eclipse, because of the danger – "it left black holes in your eyes."[19] Like the immovable summer sun perched high in a cloudless blue sky, the setting of her third novel, *À ciel ouvert* (Breakneck), Arcan shone brightly. She scattered light all around her. She did what she faulted our contemporary world for: aimed a spotlight at existence. Television and computer screens, fashion photography, film cameras, webcams . . . so many eyelids open on the world, in such a way that details and contours are erased. The fascism of being "all-seeing" results in obliteration. This is what Nelly Arcan put on display. She was the image that gives itself entirely and saturates the gaze. And what was seen when we looked at her? What was seen in this blinding glare?

À ciel ouvert is a hell on Earth. In it, Arcan describes a sun so close to Earth that everything disappears in a hyper-brightness, the devil's light that burns humans, making the capacity of seeing (seeing everything, like Rose's surgically altered genitals shown at the end of the novel) a death sentence. Seeing everything is an experience impossible to manage. A female sex waxed, stripped, is a trap-image, a hole one falls into, like in a postmodern version of Gustave Courbet's 1866 painting *The Origin of the World*. In Arcan's world, woman is no longer a dark continent; she is a crudely sutured one.

Light always seeks more light. Seeing is never done seeing. And if seeing is inexhaustible, it is because something always remains hidden. Like the whore who does not reveal her name, does not tell her life story, does not kiss, Nelly Arcan does not give it all away. Her blondness is a subterfuge. At the Cinéma L'Amour, it is not the image on the screen that interests her, but rather the sounds of men masturbating, little noises that rise out of the dark, like little lights. Like the "aurora borealis I kept hidden to paper over the faces of my clients when they tried to get too close."[20] In this darkness Nelly Arcan becomes a *luciola* – whore and firefly, whore and usherette, the girl who leads moviegoers to their seats using a little flashlight pointed at the floor.

Nelly Arcan's *luciola*:

> Whores, like Internet girls, [are] sentenced to die by their own hand because they spent the vital energy of their young years too fast, they preferred to finish themselves off, feeling the roar of the final miles instead of crawling through the remains of existence. By killing themselves they were like the light of dead stars reaching us in the lag of their explosion, light the astronomers say is the most dazzling of all because at the moment of death, they give up the best part of themselves, like hanged men.[21]

Fireflies cannot be observed under a spotlight; they can only be seen "in the present of their survival."[22] As Georges Didi-Huberman recounts in *Survivance des lucioles* (Survivings of the fireflies),[23] Pier Paolo Pasolini mourned the passing of humans. And yet, he adds, Pasolini was aware of their survival, as was Nelly Arcan, who was described as a black diamond – that rare diamond of mysterious origin, which, some contend, results from the shock of an encounter between Earth and a supernova. Nelly Arcan, therefore, is like the myth of the virgin birth, out of this world, a natural, interstellar phenomenon. This is how she resists. She allows us to see the tiny lights that nonetheless remain, fireflyimages bordering on disappearance. For if Nelly Arcan's novels play with full-on luminosity (saying everything, showing everything), really they are pleas against too much lighting, the society of the spectacle and its inherent cynicism: "With me writing meant opening the wound, it meant betraying, it meant writing what was missing, the story of scars, the fate of the world when the world has been destroyed."[24]

◦ ◦ ◦

Nelly Arcan takes us to movie theatres, bars, after-hours clubs, bedrooms, into the labyrinth of the web. She is our usherette through obscurity, opening her legs all the way to Japan to show us where to go, how to look for white spots in the darkness of waste. Like in this scene from *Hysteric*: "Staring at the glass bowl, I saw the abortion had borne fruit, and the baby had grown back. In the red of the blood I sought the white blotch."[25] Despite her apparent flamboyance, Nelly Arcan is in the image of that light – fleeting, a *passante* (passerby, like in Baudelaire's poem *À une passante* [To a passerby]) with a flickering presence. A wandering soul, like those faces Didi-Huberman pinpoints in Botticelli's drawings for *The Divine Comedy*, "small painful glimmer of the sins crawling under endless accusation and punishment."[26] Like the souls Marilyn Monroe used to imagine seeing in the lights of Los Angeles, thrashing in the night, lost souls wandering in the City of Angels, stranded between hell and purgatory.[27] Nelly Arcan is one of those fireflies that "endure, in their very bodies, eternal and mean burning,"[28] tiny ghosts "luminescent, dancing, erratic, elusive, robust."[29]

If fireflies are fated to disappear in the blinding light, then humans are "defeated, annihilated, pinned up or dried up under the artificial light of projectors, under the panopticon eye of surveillance cameras, under the deadly restless glow of television screens."[30] This is why Nelly Arcan must be seen as a desiccated butterfly, a sacrificed pin-up, a dead star in the literary heavens. And this continues beyond her death. Unpublished writing is made public in the same way as there was an attempt to screen the completed footage of *Something's Got to Give*, even as 20th Century Fox continued denying its existence. In the same way, fragments of texts written by Marilyn Monroe have just been published. What light is to be shed here, and directed at what? What is to be made blond and shiny? What darkness is to be extinguished, and what silence suppressed? What is being sought in those posthumous film clips, when the film strip runs out and the screen fills with twinkling dots, when the blond hair keeps shining beyond death?[31]

In her last movie, Marilyn "was in top form" – "every time she appeared, the screen exploded with light."[32] And it has often been repeated that, on the eve of her death, Nelly Arcan was saying she wanted children.

○ ○ ○

It's as though we had been fooled. Who was Nelly Arcan? The drama of her death deprived us of something we never had, or even worse, we held the one we loved so tightly that we smothered her – like a firefly in a jar, or a butterfly pinned to a board. And do we not also bear the guilt, like Monroe's psychoanalyst Ralph Greenson, of not saving her with our love? Or, no doubt also like him, of having been fascinated by her, but not truly loving her? Do we not share the shame of consuming her unscrupulously, like Monroe, that blond with a "lost soul"[33] who used to say that she belonged to "whoever wants to have a piece of me"?[34] In a telegram to Robert Kennedy, Monroe apologized for her absence at a political event: "I AM INVOLVED IN A FREEDOM RIDE PROTESTING THE LOSS OF THE MINORITY RIGHTS BELONGING TO THE FEW REMAINING EARTHBOUND STARS. AFTER ALL, ALL WE DEMANDED WAS OUR RIGHT TO TWINKLE."[35]

Nelly Arcan also claimed the right to twinkle. Perhaps she was expecting from us what we always expect from people we love – to be loved without being used. If Truman Capote was right and love is the meeting of two "walking wounds . . . [t]wo incomplete beings searching for something they'll never be able to find in another person,"[36] the relationship between Nelly Arcan and her audience could only match the image of our failed love affairs. And is it not this impossible relationship and its ensuing inescapable pain that, in the end, her novels put into words? One of the sentences Nelly Arcan retains from Schneider's novel is the one Marilyn wrote in the margin of *Civilization and Its Discontents*: "Loving someone means giving them the power to kill you."[37] Are we Nelly Arcan's tomb? Were we her tormentors? And now, what are we doing with her legacy?

Ralph Greenson, when asked what he remembers most about Marilyn Monroe, replied: "Not her image . . . not that vision that made me look away and hurt as only real beauty can. Not her image, no – her voice. That melancholic, ghostly voice."[38] Schneider describes Marilyn's arrival at the fundraiser organized by the Democratic Party in May 1962, how Peter Lawford introduced her upon her arrival on the Madison Square Garden stage with this slip of the tongue: "The late Marilyn Monroe." "The audience laughs in the shadows. Marilyn has kept the promise she and Truman Capote had made: to be late for their own funeral."[39] In other words: surviving it.

Marilyn's chronic lateness, her refusal to be on time (which Arcan mentions in her review of the novel), is also a refusal to be ensnared. The expression of a resistance. Being late is a way of making others want you, desire you, wait for you, but it is also, albeit only for a while, a way of not being part of things. Being late is like flashing, appearing, disappearing, appearing, disappearing. And is arriving late not the legacy of pain for the survivors of someone who commits suicide? In that other sentence noted by Nelly Arcan in Schneider's novel (words this time from Arthur Miller), she sowed something for us: "A suicide kills two people . . . that's what it's for!"

○ ○ ○

From now on, it is our own disappearance we are fighting as we seek to survive Nelly Arcan's death. We got there too late, Arcan tells us; the writer was already dead. While all along, due to the irritation caused by the confusion between the woman and the written word, between the writer and her work, we berated her for being too alive.

Yet Nelly Arcan was seeking simply to survive. And ever since her death, Montreal has, like L.A., become the city of angels. It is Nelly Arcan's blond angel I run into everywhere. Nelly Arcan as Gorgon . . . whose stare petrifies me through the mirror image of all the sacrificed blonds she reflects back to me. The angel who whispers the sentence haunting the literary heavens ever since Roland Barthes wrote it (in 1967) and which Nelly Arcan, this time as Sphinx, repeats like an enigma: "The birth of the reader must be at the cost of the death of the Author."

Mural in Williamsburg, New York, featuring publicity artwork from the HBO TV series, Girls,
photograph by Charles Dyer, 2012

16

Girls 1

We kill blonds, as did Hitchcock,[1] and do away with women's power only to resurrect them (as much as is feasible) as authors, to rid us of the guilty feelings for unscrupulously consuming them as objects. But we also kill the author, the blond author, and then sadly miss her with impunity, incapable of admitting that her dazzling blondness undermined our belief in her talent. . . .

Could this explain the publication of Marilyn Monroe's *Fragments* (2012), facsimiles and transcriptions of her poems, notebooks, and letters along with photos of her, book in hand? The blond was killed but resurrected as writer, so as to close the gap between image and word, to clothe appearances with meaning; also to demonstrate the actress's depth – thus explaining her distress – as well as to cleanse our consciences for participating in her slow death sentence. Marilyn Monroe was no fool; she understood the world she was moving through. Shifting her into the world of letters means not only reinventing her as an intellectual, which she likely was not[2] (at least not to the exclusion of everything else she truly was), but also refusing to acknowledge how lethal the world of images is for women, and how Marilyn Monroe was neither the first nor the last to pay the price.

Young American director Lena Dunham refuses to pay the price. Discovered by HBO in 2012–13, creator of and actress in the TV series *Girls*, Lena Dunham, if she is part of the series of young blonds streaming across our screens, throws a wrench in the works of representation. Taking the *show* out of *showgirls*, she gives us *girls*, somewhere between *Sex and the City*, cyberporn, reality TV shows (current site par excellence for the commodification of serial girls – Kim Kardashian, Paris Hilton, French TV's Nabilla, and others), and the stories of girl gangs, rebels, delinquents, outlaws (as also seen in *Heathers* [1988], *Bad Girls* [1999–2006], *Foxfire* [1996], *Thelma and Louise* [1991] . . . through to Sofia Coppola's *The Bling Ring* [2013]).

o o o

The series focuses on four friends whose names are all alliterations: Hannah Horvath, Marnie Michaels, Jessa Johansson, and Shoshanna Shapiro. They are in their early twenties, starting out in life. We see them *together* – on the street, in the park, at a party, in each other's apartments. Size, shape, hair length and colour, style, attitude, speech . . . barely different one from the other, yet just different enough. In a bonus track on the HBO-produced DVD, the four actresses are shown discussing the series, introducing their respective characters, describing these *girls*. At times it is not easy to distinguish who is speaking or about whom, if it is the actress or her character, and in the end, what we have are four girls portraying four girls, which, already, adds up to eight.

Somewhere between *Seinfeld*, *Sex and the City*, and *The L Word*, *Girls* is the work of Dunham. There is a bit of everything in *Girls*: the friendship and the "nothing happens" characteristics of *Seinfeld*,[3] the feminine world and (more or less explicit) sex of *Sex and the City* and *The L Word*, and, of course, New York City.[4] Brooklyn, especially. Contrary to the (big) girls of *Sex and the City*, who stroll the brightly lit canyons of the urban hypostasis that is Manhattan, Dunham's *girls* most often move about in impersonal streets, industrial lofts, and ordinary apartments: "It's like we're all slaves to this place that doesn't even really want us."[5]

White, middle-class, early twenties, they do not represent *everybody*, *all* girls, but a privileged, white, invisible majority (it has been said of Dunham that hers is a "cinema of unexamined privilege"):[6] American *college girls* from proper families. Like each one of her friends, Lena Dunham's character Hannah Horvath is portrayed as a point of identification for girls "as they really are."[7]

o o o

Girls, the title Dunham chose for her series, is a meta-title, an abstraction. A title that is basically nothing more than a category: the category "girls." Brazen, iconoclastic, irreverent, unpredictable, imperfect, and awkward, they move through life one little fail at a time: "I think that I may be the voice of my generation," Hannah says to her parents, ". . . or at least *a* voice of *a* generation."

While the girls of *Girls*, like the girls in DIM pantyhose ads, form an ensemble (an all-*girl* one), Dunham says that the girls are more than the title. That members of this class of girls, of this group, will never be understood within it. Therefore, the notion of homogeneity (the "all for one" of the *Girls* ensemble) is misleading. The gap separating the *girls* from one another, that little thing that differentiates them, implies the space between each *girl* and herself – Rimbaud's "I is another" that fuses their identity. Despite appearances, *girls* are happily part of a category from which they will always break away. They are in the margins of their own ensemble, searching, failing, their identities eluding them. Therein resides their power, as does the power of *serial girls*.

Dunham notes that the *girls* will age but that the title will not change. Like a garment that one must squeeze into though it is no longer the right size and that, over time, goes out of style. We can imagine the *girls* at 30, 40, 50, still playing the same roles, eternal hipsters who have turned into *The Golden Girls*. These girls are *girls* and will stay that way. They will not become *ladies*.

Witness this discussion over a book Hannah and Shoshanna have read, *Listen Ladies: A Tough Love Approach to the Tough Game of Love*. The following exchange centres around that title (yet another title):

> Hannah: Who are "the ladies"?
> Shoshanna: Obvi we're the ladies.
> Jessa: I'm not the ladies.
> Shoshanna: Yeah, you're the ladies.
> Jessa: I'm not the ladies!
> Shoshanna: Yes, you are. You're the ladies.
> Jessa: You're being unfair. You can't force me to be a lady.
> Shoshanna: I'm not forcing you to be a lady. You just – Okay, I'm a lady, she's a lady, you're a lady, we're the ladies.[8]

Shoshanna then starts reading passages out loud from the relationship advice book, including this one: "Sex from behind is degrading, point-blank. You deserve someone who wants to look in your beautiful face, ladies." Later on, a furious Jessa comments to Hannah about that passage: "That woman is a horrible lady. . . . I'm offended by all the supposed-to's. I don't like women telling other women what to do or how to do it or when to do it. Every time I have sex, it's my choice."

So, it's *girls* against *ladies* (that set category filled with fixed meaning), the becoming-girl versus the being-lady.

The series asks, "What do girls lose if they become ladies?" Or, rather, "What do they gain other than the right to tell girls how to behave?" Does this mean that the nineteenth-century conflict between the sex worker and the lady, wife, and mother is alive and well today?

o o o

In Dunham's world, the ladies that the girls are opposed to are the same four from *Sex and the City*, and this intertext is established as early as the first episode, as noted by several critics.[9] There are inevitable comparisons to make: from the outset, a huge poster dominates the studio of Shoshanna-the-groupie, who at once compares herself, as well as her cousin Jessa, to characters in the sister series. However, this intertext is promptly dropped, and nothing will further connect the two series' characters other than their gender and New York City.

The *Sex and the City* girls, with their lives narrated by the Carrie Bradshaw voiceover recounting each episode and ending with a moral of the story like a modern-day LaFontaine,[10] know what they are looking for in the glamourama of New York: a man, money, and style. Over the years, the more status and buying power they gain, the more weight they lose. Progressively thinner and high-end, Carrie and her friends offload pounds and their original trademark single-girl status. They come to represent a crystallized identity: that of a woman who exists only in terms of coupledom, and whose mind is primarily focused on men. New York is her El Dorado.

It could be said that, at the beginning, *Sex and the City* seemed to convey feminist content: women talked and acted in a way intended to carve out some room to manoeuvre within the dominant sexual economy – in other words, the masculine one – by playing with the single's life the *way men do*. Originally they may have been *filles publiques*, working girls, free-spirited, rebellious, upfront, orgasmic, who, as Jessa in *Girls* wishes, chose when, how, and with whom they had sex. Unfortunately, with time *Sex and the City* outed itself as a veritable *becoming-lady*: the carrot dangling at the end of the stick of life was sex, that is to say (heterosexual) marriage, that is to say reproduction.

In *Girls*, the true love bond is between the girls themselves, these somewhat lost girls who live in slightly dreary places, wear poor-quality clothes on their not-quite-mannequin-looking bodies – bodies that do not conform to other male desires fabricated by the masculine. And New York City is their jungle.

Sex and the City characters are stereotypes: the blond bombshell (Samantha Jones), the traditional, prudish brunette (Charlotte York), the ambitious, emancipated redhead (Miranda Hobbes), and especially the ordinary blond, the girl next door around whom they all revolve: Carrie Bradshaw. . . . These women are women the way we like them, meaning without loving them *completely*. "Love is never directed toward this or that property of the loved one. . . . The lover wants the loved one *with all of its predicates*, its being such as it is,"[11] writes Agamben. And if, as he suggests, when we love, we love the *whole* person, women then are not generally loved so much as loved only in fragments, in separate parts, as the ornaments they are. This is how their objectification operates. In this context, *Sex and the City* is a supermarket where everybody can find what they want at a low cost, the by-default stance being that of the narrator-writer who presents the least offensive identity possible: the average *woman*, the superwoman who has succeeded in all things, as wife and mother while being just enough of a sexy-beast, the sum total of all princesses.

In *Girls*, this site is occupied by Hannah Horvath, another writer working with autobiography, like Carrie Bradshaw. Except that Hannah Horvath's stories, when read onscreen, are either checkmated (like at the public reading she gives of a few lines scribbled in the subway to replace the text she had planned to read and that she discards at the last minute), or they provoke drama (like when Marnie and Charlie break up after Charlie reads Hannah's account of their relationship). Contrary to Carrie Bradshaw, Hannah Horvath gives neither examples nor lessons. She describes what she perceives as reality. And she is not as thin as a rail.

Lena Dunham, for whom hating the body is neither her cup of tea nor the cross she tries to bear, puts her body onscreen. She is accused of being chubby and not quite perfect, and she takes advantage of this to intersperse her show with scenes in which she appears naked, refusing televisual anorexia. This performance of the body, noted by all, is at the core of what *Girls* does. The controversial actress has heard it all, from applause to insults, the exhibition of her body praised in the name of women's rights and reviled on matters of taste and beauty. But in the end, this metonymic body, like Hannah's failed/botched writing, and like the series itself, says a lot.

o o o

As we know, Hollywood loves happy endings, and romantic sex, the spectacle of pretty sex, of well-choreographed, good-looking sex. Hollywood loves elegant (and therefore missionary) sex that seals true love, in the same way as those never-ending marriage proposals do: a man slips a ring on a woman's finger, a man's genitals slide into a woman's, and all is well.

As Elaine Blair writes in an article about sex in *Girls*:

> Hollywood sex scenes are typically not interested in ever hinting at the ways that people actually reach orgasm, and this is disheartening above all for female viewers, who develop a certain melancholy by the time they have seen their one thousandth sex scene in which it is taken for granted that by sex we mean mutually rapturous face-to-face vaginal intercourse.[12]

Blair focuses on a specific scene from the series' first season, in which Adam, Hannah's boyfriend, interrupts their missionary-style intercourse, removes his condom, and masturbates over her chest while fantasizing out loud: "You were a junkie and you were only eleven . . . you're a dirty little whore and I'm gonna send you home to your parents covered in cum."[13]

We don't actually see much during this scene: the camera shows their faces clearly but leaves their actions obscured. What remains are the noises Adam makes and the depiction of his orgasm. The scene ends with a close-up of Hannah's face: "That was really good. That was so good. I almost came." As she puts her clothes back on, Hannah alludes to Adam's earlier fantasy, ironically commenting that she is an eleven-year-old girl going home covered in sperm. Adam looks at her perplexed, as if he has amnesia; he cannot remember what he said or recognize his words when they are repeated to him out of context, taken out of the sexual setting. As for Hannah, she remembers everything because as a writer, she spends her time taking mental notes, ensuring that her experiences become writing material.

This scene made a lot of ink flow in the media because we never see such things on TV, and it was either rejected as inelegant, raw, and pornographic, or admired for being frank.[14] In fact, to be honest, it is easier and safer to oppose Adam's sexuality (to be offended by it, or to trash it) than to identify with Hannah's point of view, she who experiences this scene on a secondary level, without completely leaving herself behind, because she is there in the same way that we read a book, willingly suspending disbelief without forgetting that it is fiction. What *Girls* ends up showing are the real fifty shades of sexuality – something that is impossible in Hollywood:

Pornography depends, as we know, on showing sexual acts other than intercourse, since intercourse inconveniently hides a lot of the hot throbbing action. Hollywood films are, on the whole, anti-pornographic, in the sense that, in spite of their supposed interest in titillating their audience, they are almost uniformly content with the suggestion that couples are having vaginal intercourse – no more, no less. So there you go: a dose of porn, judiciously applied by an extremely intelligent director can save cinematic sex. I wouldn't have believed it if I hadn't seen it on *Girls*.[15]

Sexuality abounds in *Girls*, like in porn films where sex scenes (as Linda Williams has shown)[16] occur along stylistic themes and variations common to musical comedies. There is some of this in Dunham's work. The sex scenes – acrobatic, playful, clinical, weird, devoid of romantic intent – do recall the porn genre. Sex comes with no strings attached, or almost none. It happens differently each time, yet always as if detached from reality. If sex moves the plot forward, it does so as a gap, an ellipsis that suspends the narrative. It acts as an interlude and a springboard from which the girls can jump in order to occupy new places or be reborn, like a phoenix.

That is the interest of the sex seen in *Girls*, which, like Dunham's body, is distributed throughout. Sex is everywhere, it overflows, it occupies the televisual space and does so like a question (not like an answer, nor a resolution). Contrary to what we are usually given (sexuality focused on male sex and desire, following the usual hardcore porn codes), here sex is girls' sex, and it is a measure of who they are. In the same way that who they are is neither something they know nor an enigma they strive to resolve ("I am busy trying to become who I am,"[17] Hannah says nonsensically), sex is not a sure thing, either. Or rather, it is not an activity that matters in the same way as trying to discover who they are. At any rate, no more and no less than the rest. As Elaine Blair puts it: "For all its emphasis on sexual and romantic experience, *Girls* never suggests that a smoothly pleasant sex life is something worthy of serious aspiration."[18]

What *Girls* shows us, through Hannah and Adam's relationship, is nothing unique in real life. But it is something never or seldom seen onscreen. In fact, Hannah has understood everything: she has understood that this is a porn script, a fantasy, and that all of this does not define her, that she can play with it.

Therein lies the cornerstone of this TV series: the irony that liberates serial girls.

Girls, photograph by Peter Dutton, 2013

17

Girls 2

The television series *Girls* – much like Hannah's obsessive-compulsive behaviour, where she must repeat her actions eight times to counter her anxiety – has everything to do with serial reproduction. The reproduction of girls, white, middle-class girls who suffer from anxiety produced, at least in part, by seriality itself. Anxiety is expressed throughout the episodes: the girls who are asking not only what kind of world we live in, a world in which they participate and which they take a hard look at, but also what it means to be someone, what is the basis of singularity, where do we see ourselves fit in terms of the expectation to be *like all girls*. In the second season, the emphasis is on irony (that citational posture allowing the girls to take on the prevailing working order all the while rejecting it, in a kind of splitting of personal experience). The emphasis is also on images of repetition multiplying as episodes unfold, like a *mise en abyme* of seriality itself, up to and including the heroine's own obsessive-compulsive disorder. Displays of objects in drugstores and hardware stores, groups of girls sitting on park benches who duplicate the *girls* themselves, almost-identical boy characters like the AndrewAndrew DJ duo seen in the first episode (the place of men in the episodes could be equated with the Bond girls in James Bond movies!). . . . Everything here has to do with "reality" and its representation. The irony is that it is impossible to distinguish the original from the copy. The girls are constantly moving from one level to the next in search of a truth that does not exist. There is no original, nor is there a copy: the world we live in is, largely, a world of clones.

This would seem to be the meaning of the episode in which Hannah finds herself in the brownstone of a forty-something doctor, played by handsome actor Patrick Wilson. Seduced by the impeccable decor right out of a Nancy Meyers movie, Hannah eventually admits that, like everybody else, she too wants to be happy. The two-day holiday with this man (more like an extended one-night stand), spent eating, playing, having sex, stirs in her the desire to have a nice house, a good-looking lover, to get married and sample fifteen different kinds of wedding cake for the banquet that will follow the ceremony. Hannah confesses these desires to her lover in a scene where it is hard to tell whether she is joking or being sincere, or if she has gotten caught up in a game of sincerity. What had seemed like a bubble of happiness quickly bursts. The doctor proves impervious to Hannah's sensitivity and suddenly becomes almost nervous about her presence in his home. He rushes back to work the next morning; Hannah wakes up alone and experiences the house as a kind of voyage through the world of adults who "own their own trashcan."[1] A world she will leave behind with little regret after putting everything back in its place, as would a tourist happy to be heading home after an exotic trip. A world that, in the end, is not for her.

This dreamlike episode highlights the series' most important aspect: the issue of capitalism and the consuming of objects as of people. "Everyone's a dumb whore," Shoshanna shouts after arriving at Jessa's wedding in the final episode of the first season. And Adam says to Hannah: "You should never be anyone's fucking slave."[2] Marnie, who has lost her job in an art gallery (her boss preferring to keep an employee with less experience but whom she is sleeping with), becomes a restaurant hostess, therefore resigning herself to a "pretty person job" and wearing a uniform that prompts Ray to say she looks like "a slutty Von Trapp child."[3] Hannah condemns Marnie's choice, asserting that she herself has never tried to use her sexuality to earn money (although she has just agreed to write an e-book in one month, in return for an advance). As for Jessa, who has impulsively married one of the few businessmen who made a profit during the financial crisis, she throws his banal life back at him: when they separate, she screams at him that being with her will have been the most exciting experience of his life. In reply, Thomas-John accuses her of marrying him for his money and, in the heat of the argument, lets slip his preference for prostitutes because they, at least, work in an honest way.

As episodes unfold, examples abound of human relationships based on commodification . . . all the characters end up resembling one another in a catalogue of everyday prostitution. Shoshanna leaves Ray because he lacks ambition, Marnie falls in love with Charlie again because he has succeeded with an app (inspired by their breakup), Hannah makes herself sick trying to write her e-book, Jessa disappears after criticizing her father for his absence all her life (meanwhile, he now lives in the country, where he raises and eats only rabbits!). The fact of perhaps having been victims of childhood sexual abuse (if we believe Jessa's and Hannah's accounts) as much as their sexual encounters depicted as endless power games (between Adam and Natalia, Elijah and Marnie, Marnie and Booth Jonathan, Hannah and Laird . . .) highlights a social economy in which individuals, more specifically girls, are either expected to sell themselves or are perceived as whores: "I can like your cock and *not* be a whore,"[4] Natalia says to Adam when he attempts to transpose their sexual encounter into a porn story, like he had previously done with Hannah.

These anecdotes all seem to suggest that in the adult world, *every-body* is a whore. Therefore, if the goal pursued by the *Sex and the City* women, perpetually hanging out and questing for designer shoes, was full participation in the prevailing capitalist system (prostitution here taking on the conventional acceptable traits of marriage),[5] the *girls*, for their part, make a deliberate detour, resisting human trafficking even when they seem to be participating. Here, common slavery and everyday commodification are offset by their inclination for what they call *experi-ence*. "I want to feel everything,"[6] Hannah says, meaning she doesn't want to indulge in the trivial, where normal life is put on display. If the girls are part of a lost generation, it is lost because it is trying to survive, because it prefers not to buy into the market that makes up the world, a world in which *serial girls* are one of the cornerstones.

But actually, the *girls* are not that lost. When Marnie bursts out laughing when her artist-lover Booth Jonathan suggests she focus on a doll sitting at the foot of the bed while he has sex with her, unconcerned about the pleasure she may or may not be having; when a furious Jessa smashes a trophy awarded to her rich husband for his "humanitarian work"; when Shoshanna criticizes her boyfriend Ray for his cynical view of the world and leaves him in order to preserve a certain naivety; when Hannah awkwardly reclaims her life through the OCD she suffered from as a teen . . . the series demonstrates how the girls are trying to escape repetition, to resist the mainstream that urges them to become copies. In other words: *serial girls*. They are saved by accident, by anger, laugh-ter, excess – not by what singles them out, shifting them from being the same to being different, but by the very act of differentiation, one that signifies a constant, boundless *becoming*.

Solitude has a price, as does gregariousness. These girls' place in the world resembles a couples' date being crashed by an army of single women: single, as they usually are during the series, refusing domestica-tion. The *girls* are single, and they are so in a manner echoing Melville's famous character Bartleby.[7]

o o o

Deleuze writes of Bartleby that he is without referent, without ties, that he stands alone, that he speaks incomprehensibly in a language wholly contained in one phrase: "I would prefer not to."[8] Bartleby neither agrees nor disagrees; he neither accepts nor refuses hegemony. Simply, he stays in the background. This explains why, according to Slavoj Zizek,[9] it is necessary to imagine Bartleby in power: his formula is what remains of the revolution once you have refused to participate in the resistance mechanisms co-opted by the society of the spectacle that return the powers that be into place. Bartleby's "I would prefer not to" is not a retreat from reality (which an outright refusal would be, for example); rather, it is an acceptance that keeps one foot in refusal. There is no violence in Bartleby's behaviour – or, if there is, it resides in his insistence, the fact that he *stays* there. Actually, we might be relieved if he said no, because we would then get a sense of what is what. What is unbearable is the fact that he does not completely refuse, and so, as Deleuze writes, Bartleby earns the right to survive.

But Bartleby also signifies resistance to Wall Street in the face of growing industrialization and the ensuing questions concerning slavery. Neither depressed nor melancholy, Bartleby could be said to be the one who knows the meaning of reproducing; he understands what seriality means. While he does not withdraw, while he continues to take part, his "I would prefer not to" signals a retreat, the figure of someone who knows what world he is dealing with. Bartleby is not naive; he does not shut his eyes on the consumer reality that turns humans into commodities. Nor do Lena Dunham's *girls*.

o o o

This is why we must imagine Bartleby as a girl, one who, like him, speaks a language that simultaneously ebbs and flows, that neither agrees nor disagrees, that is made of driftings and deviations (such as Hannah saying to her parents: "I am busy trying to become who I am."). A girl who is at once the voice of her generation and *a* voice of *a* generation ("I may be the voice of my generation, or at least *a* voice of *a* generation," Hannah says). A girl who survives by whirling about in a suspense that keeps everyone at bay. A girl who does not hesitate to be part of a series because it is a rite of passage of femininity, and who finds in strategic seriality (in the sense that Diana Fuss, in *Essentially Speaking*, talks of strategic essentialism)[10] an exit.

Lena Dunham's *girls* prefer not to be *ladies*, those women who know things once and for all and who succeed in life. The *girls* do not seek to occupy the place reserved for them in the world within the series; rather, they move forward, individually and together, one faux pas after another.

The girls are the traps set for slippery things, the "I would prefer not to" that upsets the comforting harmony of an order that makes women's bodies a permanent spectacle, a butcher's stall display, an exhibition hall, an auction, prisoners in front of a firing squad. It is against this fascism that the girls prefer to disperse, spilling out in all directions.[11]

From this point of view, Bartleby's "I would prefer not to" is a bracketing of self rather than the hope of someday discovering *who we are*, once we have acknowledged that identity is nothing more than a label glued to our forehead. This is why I want to see the girls as a community of celibates, and even more: as the Trojan horse of becoming-single(s) that feminism needs today.

From the film *Sarah préfère la course*, 2013, © La Boîte à Fanny

18

Street Girls

I n Chloé Robichaud's film *Sarah Prefers to Run* (2013), Sarah, the film's heroine, has all the makings of a Bartleby. Quiet, introverted, often speechless, Sarah's face gobbles up the whole screen, and her enormous Nadia Comaneci eyes[1] convey a perpetual questioning. Yet one thing is certain: while we don't know much about Sarah, we do know she *prefers* to run. Which means that she *prefers not to* do everything else. And it is true: Sarah runs like she breathes. She runs whenever possible, on the track as well as on the street. And she is not alone. The tracking shots, Sarah's teammates, close-ups of feet (and the importance of the shoe motif, from running shoes to high heels), rhythmic footstep sounds . . . all represent sport as a place of seriality. Because not only does Sarah run, she is also part of an all-girls' team, whose main goal is to be the first across the finish line.

But there is more to it: when Sarah runs, she runs away from something, she escapes. Like Bartleby, she is unattached, deeply alone. She can't explain why she prefers to run, just as she couldn't say why she doesn't enjoy sex with the man she married in order to access student loans and grants. She is not without desire; rather, she struggles with a wordless desire, a desire that is also "on the run."

Sarah prefers to run, and Chloé Robichaud, for her part, prefers a slow pace. The contrast is striking: the difference between the speed of the feet on the track and the slow takes, how the camera lingers on faces, the attention to detail that slows down the image. . . . A difference like the one Sarah constantly experiences; she is always behind or ahead, as are the other girls, who bear little difference from her. Even the film's ending, suggesting that Sarah chooses to continue to run (despite a heart condition), leaves the viewer dangling: Chloé Robichaud keeps us in the starting blocks before the whistle blow; she shows neither the finish line, nor the race result, nor the chosen object of sexual desire (does Sarah prefer girls over boys?). *Sarah Prefers to Run* maintains the precarious balance implied by the chosen verb: *to prefer*. That is how she stands out within the series that she nevertheless belongs to, a series of girls who prefer to run – that is to say, they prefer not to stay still.

Therefore, if Sarah/Chloé Robichaud has a preference for running, then she also prefers *the street*, in the sense that this choice is about showing girls in motion, girls moving forward in the outside world, and for whom enclosed places – apartments, kitchens, beds – are always too small. These girls who run are girls on a femininity strike, in the sense that they are against a femininity that defines itself in (and as) domestic space, which Robichaud, in turn, defines as feminine. Sarah constantly leaves her *place*, just like her coach, who tells Sarah that she has been married and divorced three times against her mother's wishes and who prefers to invest in home landscaping instead of helping her daughter out financially. Sarah takes risks, puts herself in danger. If her concern is not political in terms of governmentality – Sarah fights to keep running, but shrugs off any other kind of commitment – it is political in terms of identity. The film asks: What happens when a girl starts to run? What does it mean when a girl takes to the street?

○ ○ ○

I began this book in reaction to Quebec's spring 2012 protests, when students and then parts of the whole population took to the street. When we marched through Montreal shouting, "Who owns the streets? We own the streets!" Today I question the meaning of this *we*. Who is this *we*? And which streets are we talking about? Under what circumstances, and at what cost? Today I wonder whether the streets also belong to women. . . .

I am thinking here of Sofie Peeters's documentary, which aired on social media and then on Belgian television in 2012. In the film, a hidden camera follows Peeters down the streets of Brussels, and as she walks, we hear salacious comments, whistles, catcalls, and insults uttered behind her back. Whore, cunt, ugly bitch. The documentary is called *Femme de la rue* (Woman of the street). It is said that when women are on the street, it is not simply to exist but to do something or to go somewhere. That, contrary to men, they do not have the "right" to be in public space. That to do so is risky, and the risk incurred is to become a "public woman." The woman who doesn't move, explains sociologist Irene Zeilinger, makes herself available, because basically, the streets belong to men.

Women's place in public space varies from one geographical location (country, city) to another, and it would be dangerous to confuse them all (scenes from Sofie Peeters's film are replayed in a documentary made in the streets of Paris for the French TV show *Envoyé spécial* [Special reporter];[2] the scenario is necessarily different, as it would be, for better or worse, anywhere in the world). Nevertheless, one general truth remains for the majority of women: the wariness about the street that girls are taught from infancy. The story of Little Red Riding Hood is never far from our consciousness, and what remains for a woman is constant awareness of imminent danger related to – almost essentially in the social landscape and gender relationships – being perceived (by others and by herself) as prey. Something like what Marie Cardinal expressed in *In Other Words*: "An ant can rape her."[3] And this is echoed, revisited, in Virginie Despentes' *Baise-moi* (Fuck me): "I leave nothing precious in my cunt for those jerks."[4]

The danger of being sweet-talked, then insulted. The danger of being felt up or rubbed up against on public transit. The danger of being raped, beaten, and left for dead. And with the danger comes risk-taking. This risk is what interests me. The risk incurred by women when they take to the streets. When they shout: "We own the streets!"

o o o

During 2012, in the wake of various "Springs" (in Egypt, Tunisia, Syria, Quebec, Greece, Spain, Turkey, Brazil . . .), we have seen a rise of feminism in public space – or at least its media coverage. In step with Lady Godiva, the suffragettes, the Mothers of the Plaza de Mayo, the civil rights protesters, and 1970s prochoice and anti-sexism feminists, "rebel women" – *Les insoumises*, as the *Courrier International* headline ran[5] – feminists have taken to the streets. And the streets now include the web, social media, and everything that so-called 2.0 technology has made possible for the monitoring, vigilance, denunciation, organization, display, and demonstration of feminist interests.

The Arab Women's Revolution, the Quebec Spring's student strikers (as well as the *Mères en colère et solidaires,* a parallel movement of mothers on strike in solidarity with Quebec students, activists from women's centres, social workers, teachers working at various grade levels . . .), the events surrounding Pussy Riot's performance and sentencing, the Femen movement, Idle No More, women calling for a national inquiry into missing and murdered Aboriginal women, #blacklivesmatter. . . . Everywhere, women are protesting: naming, telling, revealing, condemning this protracted death sentence – a pervasive, ordinary, insidious, perverse femicide. Countless deeds that, to paraphrase Judith Butler, transform the human being's constitutive precariousness into an unbearable one.[6]

For women, that is, for those who are said to be women, apparently recognized and identified as such,[7] the streets have not been won. A room of one's own, so necessary at the beginning of the twentieth century (clearly for the economic freedom it represented, but mostly for the freedom to think), has become a prison. Nowadays it is the streets that women must take back – as in these anti-processions (to use Virginia Woolf's image in *Three Guineas*), such as Take Back the Night and Slutwalks, flashmobs, performances, and various occupations. Staying in the street: the ultimate feminist gesture. Daring to stay in the street.

Consequently, my question is as follows: Who owns the streets? Who are the "people" in the streets saying "we the people"? When women say "we the people," are they speaking as women? And when they say "we women," do they represent the people?

o o o

Whenever "we the people" expresses itself, not everybody is included. As Judith Butler writes in the collection *Who Is a People?*, "'we the people' always has its constitutive outside, as we know. It is thus surely not the fact that the 'we' fairly and fully represents all the people."[8] Butler examines the organic dimension of this speech act that constitutes the people, a particularly significant organic dimension when it comes to individuals faced with an accelerated precariousness and who, by taking to the street, fight against oblivion:[9] "The point is not to regard the body merely as an instrument for making a political claim but to let this body, the plurality of bodies, become the precondition of all further political claims."[10] And the plurality of bodies is linked to places: "bodies belong to the pavement, the ground, the architecture, and the technology by which they live."[11] Butler offers for consideration that popular sovereignty necessarily implies the performative affirmation of bodies:

> Bodies assemble precisely to show that they are bodies, and to let it be known politically what it means to persist as a body in this world, and what requirements must be met for bodies to survive, and what conditions make a bodily life, which is the only life we have, finally livable.... We take to the streets because we need to walk or move there; we need streets to be structured so that, whether or not we are in a

chair, we can move there, and we can pass through that space without obstruction, harassment, administrative detention, or fear of injury or death. If we are on the streets, it is because we are bodies that require infrastructural support for our continuing existence, and for living a life that matters. Mobility is itself a right of the body, to be sure, but also a precondition for the exercise of other rights, including the right of assembly itself.[12]

Which brings me to Femen, a particular case of *serial girls*. What happens when girls leave the podium and billboards and take to the streets as women? At this point I don't wish to debate for or against Femen, nor take sides on their position, be it clear or not so clear, about monotheisms, and more specifically about Islam and the wearing of the hijab (at the very least a controversial position, if not a problematic one, not only because it borders on Islamophobia but also in relation to global, intersectional feminism and the issue of women's freedom of choice). Nor do I wish to idealize Femen by presenting them as the sole model.[13] Rather, I want to focus on a very specific dimension of their mode of operation, which in my eyes is worthy of analysis: the way they occupy the streets.

As young feminist soldiers against patriarchy (media suffragettes, aspiring crypto-politicians, according to *Tecknicart* magazine),[14] as version 2.0 Amazons, Femen demonstrate against religious fundamentalism, the trafficking in and commodification of women, DSK (Dominique Strauss-Kahn), the sexual harassment of students by university professors . . . borrowing their confrontational tactics and spectacle from the military world. The difference is that instead of putting on a uniform, they take off their clothes. Their skin, and more specifically their exposed breasts, across which they write slogans, is their – fragile – uniform. For journalist Gillian Schutte, demonstrating in the nude is an act of civil disobedience within the dominant context of global misogyny. It is a way of forsaking the male libidinal economy and the world as seen by, and therefore created by (and for), the masculine gaze (this world that is therefore the street). "Women are spilling out from those margins,"[15] writes Schutte, while Alice Schwarzer adds, in the German feminist magazine *Emma*, "They are catching the boomerang in mid-air and throwing it back."[16]

Don't pose, Femen activists say, *you're not models, you're soldiers!* Against the immobility of the doll, movement: the production of the common against private interiority, and assigned identities proceeding from the exposure of intimacy (the naked skin) and biological femininity's most visible feature. There is a catch here, of course, and a risk. When bare-breasted members of Femen demonstrate wearing flower wreaths, it is advertising (the cliché, the stereotype) that is taking to the streets. Femen members' nudity is like the boomerang's return in the sense that they confront the other with his desire for female nudity, and the political meaning of his desire. They trap him, they shame him.

Moreover, Femen put themselves in physical danger. They expose themselves (breasts, belly) to reveal (unveil) the true face of those in front of them. While women who get naked in public are considered of "easy virtue," Femen test just how far the virtue of the self-righteous will go – even if this means having to suffer the consequences.[17]

So it's "we the women" who express and move ourselves out into the street, and the risk that Femen activists take involves exactly that: taking a stand in public, on the street, visible and available to all.[18] Femen expose themselves as women. Their female/feminine bodies stand up against the police force, the (discursive) political body opposing the erotic body. Slogans written directly on the skin are essential: more than an outfit, they are the body's own writing, acting as a shield against its eroticization. The words are the skin are the clothes. What about nudity, then? And which body is touched by the policemen's hands? A political body that is everything at once: symbolic, collective (that represents, that creates images) and organic, singular (that suffers, that can be hurt). As Butler writes:

> To be shorn of protection is a form of political exposure, at once concretely vulnerable, even breakable, and potentially and actively defiant, even revolutionary. . . . To show up is both to be exposed and to be defiant, meaning precisely that we are crafted precisely in that disjuncture, and that in crafting ourselves, we expose the bodies for which we make our demand. We do this for and with one another, without any necessary presumption of harmony or love. As a way of making a new body politic.[19]

Femen reclaim a space of appearance, the space needed for politics, for those whose lives are not livable, vulnerable bodies that Femen display and put into play. Borrowing from street theatre, they play on the double meaning of the word *people*. *People*: they act like celebrities. They are criticized for playing the media's game, but that is precisely their main strategy, the cornerstone of their poaching tactics, what Michel de Certeau calls "oppositional practice."[20] Femen's political body is a dialectic image, one that evokes another, and makes it tremble. Because, by climbing down off billboards, the naked girls strip *them*. It has been said that men masturbate over Femen images: I prefer to think that they rub their eyes. A Femen's body is a body we are expected to read. Skin with slogans written all over it, a performing body, in representation, in movement, a screaming body, a body that calls on us to become sensitive – politically speaking. This is where the face of the other, central to Emmanuel Levinas's thought, and the injunction it carries – "Thou shalt not kill"[21] – connect with Femen's action.

Femen's bare chest is always associated with a face (contrary to advertisements or pornography). It is neither framed nor cropped. Moreover, this face speaks. Despite what has been said, Femen is not "fast-food" feminism deriving from or linked to the world of bling and kitsch; it is the public expression of precarious lives (populations ostracized one way or another) who look at *us* and say "we the people," that is to say "we the women." Taking to the street means imposing one's body beside another body. It means refusing to be overlooked, relegated to the (supposedly inoffensive) status of image. It means to assert oneself as an integral part of this "people" in whose name one defends liberty, equality, and fraternity. . . . The Femen sorority is all about occupying a public space that belongs to women as well, but from which they have been, in countless literal or figurative ways, perpetually kept out of. Their actions make it loud and clear that "we the people" includes them too.

○ ○ ○

"We just show people what the people can do,"[22] says a Pussy Riot member now in hiding. This is where the "we, girls" of serial resistance serves the "we, women" of the ordinary world.

The example of Pussy Riot, the Russian feminist punk band prosecuted for singing a feminist prayer on the altar of the Cathedral of Christ the Saviour in Moscow, stirs up the rage of Orthodox followers.[23] This prayer was not the group's first performance, but it was the first to prompt such repression – two of the girls taken into custody have been sentenced to two years of forced labour in penal colonies. Consisting of "more than ten members,"[24] according to them, this girl band – *devushki* in Russian – organically functions without a leader, in an indivisible, anonymous, and representative manner. Balaclavas covering their heads, wearing colourful dresses and tights in child-like fashion, they stage punk performances. They write political protest songs, playing them in unlikely public places to create a surprise effect. In accordance with their band's name, Pussy Riot – "pussy" referring to a kitten and to female genitalia – they cover their tracks, pranking up the action with a girl costume both vulgar/sexual and harmless. Yet their message is clear. Against sexism, capitalism, "Putinism," they compel the public to take to the street, to occupy Red Square, to brandish its freedom and anger. They shout: "We exist!"

Pussy Riot describe themselves as "court jesters," borrowing from both clown and balladeer, voicing truths under the guise of levity. Depicted as witches, they stir things up in the public arena, and transform the Court of Justice into a theatre venue. When the Russian government sought to make an example of their trial, the Pussy Riot girls caught the ball on the rebound and sent it right back. The opening and closing statements they read at their trial (and the wild applause from the audience) attest to the power they gained in turning the tables.[25] Despite the fact that they have been sentenced for what some consider a peccadillo (the punishment is disproportionate to the crime), Pussy Riot had an undeniable public impact, mobilizing thousands of supporters all around the world.

If Pussy Riot managed to rip the Russian government's democratic mask off, they also succeeded in making the whole world wear balaclavas. Anonymity won the game when their costume went viral. We are all Pussy Riot.[26] As Slavoj Zizek says, their message is clear: ideas are what count.[27] Hence the balaclavas, masks of impersonality, symbols of a liberating anonymity. Their balaclavas impart physical reality to an idea, and that is why Pussy Riot are such a threat: it is easy to imprison individuals, but try imprisoning an idea![28]

o o o

The Russian government deemed Pussy Riot "just stupid girls"[29] and demanded that they go back to their homes. But not every girl wants to marry and have kids, claims Pussy Riot member Katya Samutsevich.

Group members who avoided arrest are now on the run, forced into hiding to escape police detection. "Putin is afraid of us," comments one of the girls. "Can you imagine? Afraid of girls?"[30] And, to paraphrase playwright Edward Albee,[31] I would add: Who's afraid of serial girls?

CBS correspondent Lesley Stahl concludes her *60 Minutes Overtime* piece on Pussy Riot with: "So, the battle of Goliath and the girls goes on,"[32] leaving us wondering who will win in the end.

Pussy Riot, photograph by Igor Mukhin, 2012

Conclusion

Firefly Girls

"We are all Pussy Riot," writes journalist Suzanne Moore in *The Guardian*.[1] And recall the words written by Marguerite Duras in *War: A Memoir* (1985): "We also belong to the same race as the Nazis."

Serial girls are at the intersection of *I* and others, fascism and revolution. Set in a pose, they stand still between disappearance and appearance, ornament and movement, domination and subversion. Serial girls captured in a freeze frame are indeed a figure: a fixed form, a stereotype, a model, a standard, a cliché. Anywhere, anytime, thinkers, artists, writers, activists, ordinary girls raise their fists to smash this illustration of *girls*, whose seriality repeatedly hammers on what we should be, what we are supposed to look like. Girls rise up against this order and, in turn, and with the use of repetition, invent new forms of resistance, other choreographies. They divert and bypass the series, reproducing it with the intention of revisiting it, of disturbing its order and identity.

The fascist part of serial girls lies in what it imposes as identity, what it gives as a model. Its counter-fascism, its resistance, its optimism, on the other hand, lies in the way this standard can be reimagined and brought to action. Serial girls refuse to stay still. They refuse the identity-based law of essentialism. They manoeuvre, lead astray, seduce as a way of setting traps, using aesthetic harmony to anaesthetize their audience, like the praying mantis does to her partner.

This is how they embody the Ungovernable.

○ ○ ○

Following Hannah Arendt, Didi-Huberman states that "within our *way of imagining* there exists, fundamentally, a condition for our *way of conducting politics*."[2] Friendly, sisterly, lustful, erotic, political ... what simultaneously unites and divides girls, what shapes their resemblance/difference, is the locus of their power. Faint glimmerings in the night sky, twinkling, ever-changing choreographies, they embody the survival that declares *girls* to be indestructible.

Girls resist. Under cover of this seriality that makes them pleasing to the eye, harmless copies of the same, their revolt brews, driven by their anger and resourcefulness. Girls resemble one another, assemble together, at times creating an impression of harmony and repetition that could recall how *girls* of all kinds, whoever and wherever they are, end up being matched together as if they were all alike, brought back to one common denominator and displayed as one series. Yet let us not be duped. While playing at serial reproduction, *girls* remain the keepers of an irreducible singularity: the very fact of being *girls*. Anonymity can act as an alibi for domestication, and being a feminist means refusing domestication, that is to say being boxed into a definition of the feminine – relegated to this Western standard of a plastic woman, white, blond, and thin. It means refusing to forget to think.

I will end with the Ungovernable and the possibility of survival *no matter what*, so as to place *serial girls* in opposition to another device: fireflies, an animal symbol that will make it possible for me to ponder the survival of *girls*, their desiring and resistant flickering.

o o o

In *Survivance des lucioles* (Survivings of the fireflies), Didi-Huberman rereads Pasolini's 1975 article, known as "Of Fireflies," and in it discerns the Italian filmmaker's pessimism, his despair at his country's neo-fascism, a despair he "illustrates" through the disappearance of fireflies in the Roman night – a fact that, he feels, must be equated with the disappearance of the *people*. What first interests Didi-Huberman in Pasolini's work is the place given to extras. He became interested in fireflies while in the process of weighing the politics of Pasolini's use of extras. During a visit to Rome some ten years later, he senses the fireflies in the darkness. Starting from this anecdote, he then counters Pasolini's claim: yes, fireflies do exist, there they are! To see them, all one needs to do is look for them. If we have all the reasons in the world to be pessimistic, then it becomes all the more urgent to look for fireflies in the night.

For Didi-Huberman, fireflies are extras and resistance fighters; they are survivings – in other words, the state of what was otherwise thought to be a disappearance. If the survivor (the individual who comes close to dying, and who survives) is the one who escapes disappearance, survivings represent a continuous state. Survivings are always there. They signal hope and, as regards power, a continual threat as well. Survivings are not essences; they are movement, flickerings, appeals. And surviving is about the singularity of what is experienced and that translates as a vibration of images. Contrary to the horizon, that dazzling promise at the end of the road, the image is a punctuation of sorts, an intermittent glimmer, a fragile "endless fluttering of appearances, disappearances, re-appearances and re-disappearances."[3] Contrary to the horizon, which is the ultimate hope for a whole – images are rifts, remains.

Capturing images: this is what Didi-Huberman has placed at the centre of his work, and what I've tried to do through *serial girls.*

Capturing girls like Baudelaire's passerby, upon whose fugitive beauty he comes to a stop, reminded of Dante's Beatrice – women seen without ever being captured. Might feminine figures, precisely because of what we invest them with, possess the potential to resist by escaping? Freeze-framed in an image of *perennial passersby*, do these girls not embody, beyond the seriality confining them, the locus par excellence of surviving?

"The first political operator of protest, of crisis, of criticism, or eman-cipation," writes Didi-Huberman, "must be called imaginary as it proves itself capable of cutting across the plane of totalitarian constructs."[4] Because, as Benjamin has shown,[5] images are a way of organizing (tak-ing apart, analyzing, contesting) our pessimism. And of making, invent-ing, imagining communities. Thus,

> In the end, the following are the fireflies' infinite resources: their retreat when it is not a strategic withdrawal into oneself but a "diago-nal force"; their clandestine community of "particles of humanity", their intermittent signals; their basic freedom of movement; their ability to make desire appear as the indestructible par excellence.[6]

o o o

The origin of the fireflies text can be found in a 1941 letter from Pasolini to Franco Farolfi, in which he tells about going into the forest with a friend one night. In this letter, infused with desire, he compares fireflies to communities of light-hearted, playful young lads. The essence of this comparison resides in "this innocent and powerful joy that rises as an alternative to moments either too somber or too bright of fascist tri-umphalism."[7] Pasolini has shifted from the erotic joy represented by the fireflies to their pessimistic disappearance in the blinding glare of pro-jectors in this society of the spectacle, of stars and *people*, of bodies exploded by light, the cinema of ordinary fascism.

But let's return to the original fireflies. We must believe in joy's sur-viving resistance, in the power of cheerful friendship and love. If imagi-nation has everything to do with our way of conducting politics, the same goes for desire. Like fireflies, whose flickering is a dance that shapes a community, girls exchange signals that register a "being together," signs of a mutual desire that links and rallies them to a shared cause: to exist.

Let's think too about the remains of the night recorded by Charlotte Beradt, scraps of dreams collected from German citizens during the rise of the Third Reich that document how the rise of totalitarianism became an obsessive fear.[8] Let's think also about accounts shared by survivors of the Shoah who speak in lieu of the dead, staying close to their experi-ence in the camps. . . . Experience may be non-translatable, its memory may fade over time; nonetheless, it can never be perfectly destroyed. Thus, as Didi-Huberman notes, even the most somber of words do not signify absolute destruction. In spite of everything, experience is inde-structible, resistant, and "surviving." It is what remains, and from what *remains* communities are forged.

o o o

Amorous flickering, therefore, flickering desire, signals sent from that "taking-place in a whatever singularity"[9] that is love. In the end, *serial girls* bring me back to the experience of love, not the candy-cane pink love we tend to associate with women as if it were a given, nor the pseudo-mystical love that too often remains a way of escaping the politi-cal. But to "love" in the sense of alliance, like the force of attraction thanks to which girls can stand together without dying because of it.

Love never binds itself to just one of the beloved's characteristics (height, blondness . . .), says Agamben; it embraces the whole.[10] *Serial girls* are *loved* as the product of a fetishism that only enhances them *in part*, that banks on their resemblance and their frozen synchronicity, on their symbolic death. But despite this enforced organizing pattern, this becoming-ornament imposed on women, I continue to think that they can nonetheless *remain* together, and that this coexistence in itself is a site of resistance, the desire for political surviving.

This book is the result of a serialization of *serial girls*, a sum of exam-ples highlighting, on the one hand, a part of the authoritarian (if not fas-cist) dimension of these images and devices, and on the other their subversive potential. Since, ultimately, I love these *serial girls*, since I am seduced by them, I can only be sensitive to their counter-power. What happens when pin-ups peel away from the calendar, when the corps de ballet of ballerinas in white tutus starts to dance in a manner as unbridled as the Black Swan, and when porn actresses choose to work behind instead of in front of the camera. What happens when feminism meets Black Panthers during a half-time show at the Superbowl, as it did when Beyoncé performed "Formation" in 2016.

Beyoncé's girls are sexualized and serialized in a way that, intelligently and subversively, draws on the Western ideal of white serial girls with which I began this book. But what they do is resist misogyny and racism by transforming the image, displacing it, multiplying it in ways that include diversity. And most importantly, by using it as a means to achieve political ends. This is why I love Beyoncé, and this is why what remains in the end, for me as for Didi-Huberman's fireflies, is a call of desire. The desire to resist together. *All for one and one for all.*

This explains why I want to hold on to the caryatids, immobilized by the roof of the Erechtheion, at an angle that turns them toward each other as in a gesture of shared support and affection. This is the reason, also, that I am holding on to Virginia Woolf's desire as infused into her *Mrs. Dalloway*, the organic yet stellar character that haunts the three women in Michael Cunningham's novel *The Hours* (1998, as well as Stephen Daldry's 2002 film version). I hold on to the kiss between Thelma and Louise before they plunge into the Grand Canyon, to the bond between Molly and Nomi (who will avenge her friend's rape) in *Showgirls*, to Sarah's feelings for her running teammates and her heart that falters as she listens to Zoey singing karaoke. I cherish the resurrection of Marilyn Monroe in the minds of so many little girls, and the luminous blond heads Nelly Arcan saved from misogyny. I share the defence of girls by girls in *The Brave One* and *Hard Candy*, Gloria Steinem's political affection for her Bunny sisters at the Playboy Club, the struggle for models' rights by former top model Sara Ziff, the team sport and the self-endangering we see in Pussy Riot and Femen. I live on the park benches, in the beds and bathtubs shared by Lena Dunham's *Girls* throughout the TV series.

I walk with Virginie Despentes' girls, and occupy the city.

I march alongside the girls on strike, and with them I resist, I refuse to retreat. . . .

○ ○ ○

In that lies the meaning of the word: *girls*. While girls are women, they are not ladies. Their resistance is not dead; they do not stop fighting against what is expected of them, the ordinary and consequently violent formatting of a becoming-ornament, of girls as ready-to-wear.

No, the *people* have not disappeared – as Pasolini feared – nor have girls. They are there, side by side, their fates linked. They are countless, and their desire is multiplied. A resistant desire that assembles, performs, ceaselessly transforms and binds them closely to one another.

The girls are alive.

Look, there they are, in the street.

They will always win over an army of dolls.

Notes

Introduction: *I* Is a Girl

1 Giorgio Agamben, *What Is an Apparatus*, trans. David Kishik and Stefan Pedatella (Palo Alto, CA: Stanford University Press, 2009), 50.

2 Thank you to Jean Bonin for this link.

1 Serial Girls

1 Marie Vlachovà and Lea Biason, eds., *Women in an Insecure World: Violence Against Women – Facts, Figures and Analysis* (Geneva: Centre for the Democratic Control of Armed Forces, 2004).

2 Annick Cojean, *Gaddafi's Harem*, trans. Marjolijn de Jager (New York: Grove Press, 2013), 77.

3 Ibid., 92.

4 I will not address here the dimension of this work that deals with international politics and a possible manipulation of public opinion in support of Western intervention in Libya. What interests me is the way in which women are portrayed in Cojean's book, and Blair's reaction to the girls.

5 From the Greek *hyphistasthai*, hypo- meaning "under" and *histasthai* meaning "support, stand."

6 Marina Yaguello, *Les mots et les femmes* (Lausanne: Payot, 1978).

7 Ibid., 179 (our translation).

8 Simone de Beauvoir, *The Second Sex*, trans. Constance Borde and Sheila Malovany-Chevalier (New York: Knopf, 2009), 5.

9 Ibid., 15.

10 I will not discuss the controversies surrounding the various archaeological and historical interpretations of these figures. For further reading, see Michael Vickers, "Persepolis, Vitruvius and the Erechteum caryatids: The Iconography of Medism and Servitude," *Revue archéologique*, vol. I (1985): 3–28.

11 Camille Paglia, "Six Headstrong Women Confidently Raise Acropolis Roof," *Bloomberg*, October 7, 2012, www.bloomberg.com.

12 See Patrick Harrop (University of Manitoba, School of Architecture), "Detached Operations: Individuation and the Modulation of Geometric Order" (unpublished manuscript, 2012).

2 Young-Girl

1 Gilles Deleuze and Félix Guattari, *A Thousand Plateaus*, trans. Brian Massumi (Minneapolis: University of Minnesota Press, 1987), 276.

2 Ibid., 289.

3 Tiqqun, *Preliminary Materials for a Theory of the Young-Girl*, trans. Ariana Reines (Los Angeles: *Semiotext(e)*, 2012), 15.

4 Ibid., 84.

3 Marginals

1 Virginia Woolf, *Three Guineas* (London: Harcourt, 1938), 18.
2 Ibid.
3 Ibid., 106.
4 Ibid., 175.
5 Ibid., 179.
6 Ibid., 227.
7 Quoted in Harold Fromm, "Virginia Woolf: Art and Sexuality," *The Virginia Woolf Quarterly Review*, summer (1979): 453.
8 Virginia Woolf, *A Room of One's Own*, cited in Ellen Hawkes Rogat, "The Virgin in the Bell Biography," *Twentieth Century Literature*, vol. 20, no. 2 (April 1974): 113.
9 Fromm, "Virginia Woolf," 456.
10 In which women are not only compared to great apes but also have their sexuality presented as a site of "scientific" investigation, to reveal not only the presence of their desire but also its polymorphic quality (the number of different objects that can arouse it), their boredom in a monogamous/conjugal context and the fact that faithfulness is not "natural" to them, and lastly their fantasies of rape and sex with strangers. . . . So many "findings" that cannot but elicit serious questions as to their political ends. See Daniel Bergner, *What Do Women Want?* (New York: Ecco, 2013).

4 From the Latin *Pupa*: Poupée, Doll, Little Girl

1 "But a little girl cannot incarnate herself in any part of her own body. As compensation, and to fill the role of alter ego for her, she is handed a foreign object: a doll. Note that the bandage wrapped on an injured finger is also called a *poupée* ['doll' in French]: a finger dressed and separate from the others is looked on with amusement and a kind of pride with which the child initiates the process of its alienation. But it is a figurine with a human face – or a corn husk or even a piece of wood – that will most satisfyingly replace this double, this natural toy, this penis." de Beauvoir, *The Second Sex*, 27.
2 Ibid.
3 See, for example, the research results of Becky Francis, "Gender, Toys and Learning," *Oxford Review of Education* 36, no. 3 (June 2010): 325–344. See also Hannah Rosin, "La fin des 'jouets de fille' et des 'jouets de garcon,'" *Slate*, December 24, 2012, www.slate.fr.
4 de Beauvoir, *The Second Sex*, 29.
5 Ibid., 30.
6 Aqua, "Barbie Girl," by Soren Rasted, Claus Norreen, René Dif, and Lene Nystrom, released May 14, 1997, on *Aquarium*, Universal MCA.
7 A medium for imitation or for subversion? asks Marie-Françoise Hanquez-Maincent about Barbie, in *Barbie, poupée totem: Entre mère et fille, lien ou rupture?* (Paris: Autrement, 1998), 120. The Mattel company is Big Sister, who "assists and monitors little girls during their lengthy and repetitive initiation into femininity, which includes the permanent need for 'aesthetic innovation' as essential component of this identity construction" (ibid., 131 [our translation]). The Barbie paradox lies precisely in her role as a model. "Isn't it the model's role to attract the other, to incite the other to imitate it, to copy it? But with Barbie, one comes up against Mattel's contradictory approach to the model. Barbie is inimitable and so by definition forever unimitated, unequalled. To imitate Barbie is to inevitably be exposed to disqualification" (ibid.).
8 G. I. Joe first existed as a character in fiction. Only later did he become a figurine, a moulded plastic version of the comic-book hero. Unlike Barbie, the G. I. Joe doll was not based on another doll (Bild Lilli), nor on a real-live girl (Barbara Handler, the Mattels' daughter). And whereas he was muscular and had moving limbs, Barbie's were de-

signed to be motionless – in other words, to pose. G. I. Joe represented all the qualities a man was expected to possess: strength, courage, vitality. But what does Barbie represent?

9 Over time, she was assigned increasingly diversified occupations, with clothes and accessories to match. But at the outset, and this is still largely true, the activities she was allowed to pursue were those traditionally associated with women (cooking, cleaning, childcare . . .) – domestic tasks or professions linked to what women are associated with: *care*.

10 This can bring to mind the political use of names in Margaret Atwood's dystopic novel *The Handmaid's Tale*, in which women are deprived of their identity to benefit a category ("the Spouses") or restricted to a property bond that makes them slaves ("Offred," i.e., "of Fred").

11 M. G. Lord, *Forever Barbie: The Unauthorized Biography of a Real Doll* (New York: Avon, 2004), viii.

12 Hanquez-Maincent, *Barbie, poupée totem*, 98 (our translation).

13 Ibid.

14 See Hanquez-Maincent, *Barbie, poupée totem*, about studies examining how children play with Barbie. This chapter seems a sort of dismissal of the guilt feeling linked to the doll so as to enhance her playful, imaginative potential. However, the fact remains that this is an adult doll, with adult contours, mainly intended for girls; the sexed, political issues are put aside in favour of a psychological reading that, in my view, overlooks certain aspects of the question. It goes without saying that the Barbie case is complex, making it impossible to draw all-encompassing general conclusions. Nonetheless, it is possible to compare the potential for play that this doll offers with the possibilities suggested by other toys in human form – Blythe, Pullip, Taeyang, and consorts. These present interesting dimensions depending on whether the body has moving joints or not, if costumes evoke an imaginary realm, if the rendering of culture, race, and gender is more or less stereotyped, and so on.

15 Lord, *Forever Barbie*, 128.

16 Mignon R. Moore, "Intersectionality and the Study of Black, Sexual Minority Women," *Gender and Society*, vol. 26, no. 1 (February 2012): 33–39.

17 Galia Slayen, "The Scary Reality of a Real-Life Barbie Doll," *Huffington Post*, April 8, 2011, www.huffingtonpost.com.

18 Hanquez-Maincent, *Barbie, poupée totem*, 23 (our translation).

19 Ibid., 28 and 36.

20 Ibid., 122.

21 Ibid., 44.

22 See Hans Bellmer's work *The Doll* (1936).

23 "To me, Barbie dies when she puts on her wedding dress," says Felicia Rosshandler, one of the artists for whom Barbie is a source of inspiration. "She never ages; she never becomes a mother." (Lord, *Forever Barbie*, 270.)

24 David Levinthal's work is interesting as it shifts from showing soldier figures in photographs, reproducing episodes of the Second World War (documented in *Hitler Moves East*), to photos of Barbie dolls: "the idea of as the Aryan virgin, and this character breaking through that." (Lord, *Forever Barbie*, 272.)

25 Hanquez-Maincent, *Barbie, poupée totem*, 86–87 (our translation).

26 Nelly Arcan, *Burqa of Skin*, trans. Melissa Bull (Vancouver: Anvil Press, 2014).

27 "Court Backs Barbie Artist in Doll of a Case," *FoxNews.com*, August 15, 2001, www.foxnews.com.

28 The Barbie Dreamhouse Experience opened near Alexanderplatz, in Berlin, in May 2013, provoking the ire of feminists. It is a pink house (which can be taken apart and

moved, with touring Europe in mind) where little girls are invited to learn to do hair and makeup, walk like models, sing like stars, or bake cupcakes.

5 Still Lifes

1 Nick Holt, *Love Me, Love My Doll* (BBC America, 2007), 50 min.
2 Ibid.
3 Ibid.
4 Catharine A. MacKinnon, *Are Women Human?* (Cambridge, MA: Belknap Press of Harvard University Press, 2006).
5 Ibid., 142.
6 Giorgio Agamben, *The Coming Community*, trans. Michael Hardt (Minneapolis: University of Minnesota Press, 1993), 63.
7 Roland Barthes, *Mythologies*, trans. Annette Lavers (New York: Noonday Press, 1972), 97–99.
8 Guy Debord, *The Society of the Spectacle*, trans. Donald Nicholson-Smith (New York: Zone Books, 1994), no. 18: 17.
9 Ibid., 36.
10 Ibid., 16.

6 Fetish-Grrrls

1 Susan Sontag, "The Pornographic Imagination," in *Styles of Radical Will* (New York: Picador, 2002 [1979]), 205–233.
2 Barthes, *Mythologies*, 147.
3 Ibid., 150.
4 As summarized by Martin Rubin in *Showstoppers: Busby Berkeley and the Tradition of Spectacle* (New York: Columbia University Press, 1993), the "Berkeleyesque" is defined by the presence of the following elements: 1) a large number of chorus girls arranged in geometric and regimented formations; 2) high-angle camera shots revealing the kaleidoscopic figures composing the displays as a whole; 3) an impression of extravagance and excess; 4) spectacular boom shots; 5) the stylized use of female bodies to create abstract shapes or to represent objects; 6) elements of erotic fetishism; 7) the use of multiple gigantic and strange accessories. Also, as Lucy Fisher explains, Berkeley not only made images of women but also made women into images. In his films, women – cut off from all identity, reduced to representing ornamental figures, in other words to acting as decor – come to represent the image itself, its essence, and woman as pure image (appearance and passivity). It bears repeating that what mattered to Berkeley was women's beauty: "I never cared whether a girl knew her right foot from her left so long as she was beautiful. . . . All my girls were beautiful and some of them could dance a little, some of them couldn't." Lucy Fisher, "The Image of Woman as Image: The Optical Politics of *Dames*," *Film Quarterly*, no. 30 (Autumn 1976): 6.
5 Siegfried Kracauer, *The Mass Ornament*, trans. Thomas Y. Levin (Cambridge, MA: Harvard University Press, 1995), 77.
6 Ibid.
7 Ibid., 78.
8 Ibid., 79.
9 Sarah Kofman, *The Enigma of Woman: Woman in Freud's Writings*, trans. Catherine Porter (Ithaca, NY: Cornell University Press, 1985), 223.
10 As Kracauer writes: "The human figure enlisted in the mass ornament has begun the *exodus* from lush organic splendor and the constitution of individuality toward the realm of anonymity to which it relinquishes itself when it stands in truth and when the knowledge radiating from the basis of man dissolves the contours of visible natu-

ral form. In the mass ornament nature is deprived of its substance, and it is just this that points to a condition in which the only elements of nature capable of surviving are those that do not resist illumination through reason" (*The Mass Ornament*, 67). See also Pascal Michon, *Rythmes, pouvoir, mondialisation* (Paris: PUF, 2005).

11 Erik Bordeleau, *Foucault anonymat* (Montréal: Le Quartanier, 2012), 12 (our translation).

12 Ibid., 28.

13 Terri J. Gordon, "Fascism and the Female Form: Performance Art and the Third Reich," *Journal of the History of Sexuality*, vol. 11, no 1–2 (January–April 2002): 164–200.

14 Gordon quotes Alfred Polgar (1968): "The obedience to invisible but ineluctable orders, the marvelous 'drill,' the submersion of the individual into the group, the concentration of bodies into a single collective 'body'" (ibid., 171–172).

15 Ibid., 172.

16 "Sturdy, blonde barbarians." Quoted in Gordon, ibid.

17 "On the surface, the production of revue girls in ornamental patterns looks very much like the political pageantry of Hitler Youth and SA men at Nazi rallies and mass marches. In his later work, Kracauer makes a direct connection between the cultural and political mass ornament, referring to the 'living ornaments' and 'tableaux vivants' of Nazi spectacle" (ibid., 184).

18 In Stany Grelet and Mathieu Potte-Bonneville, "Une biopolitique mineure. Entretien avec Giorgio Agamben," *Vacarme*, vol. 10 (Winter 2000), www.vacarme.org (our translation).

19 Milan Kundera, *The Unbearable Lightness of Being*, trans. Michael Henry Heim (New York: Harper & Row, 1984), 252.

20 A discourse he tracks in certain works produced after the war and that seek to theatricalize, from a critical viewpoint of course, the Nazi era. See Saul Friedlander, *Reflections on Nazism: An Essay on Kitsch and Death* (New York: Harper and Row, 1984).

21 Liliana Cavani, *The Night Porter*, 1974, 188 mins.

22 Susan Sontag, "Fascinating Fascism," review of *The Last of the Nuba*, by Leni Riefenstahl, and *SS Regalia*, by Jack Pia, *The New York Review of Books*, February 6, 1975, www.nybooks.com.

23 See the Disney Princess Line, created in 1999, which consists of putting all princesses in the same basket, like a single commercial brand (while ignoring the differences between them). Thus, it is now possible to find objects (over 25,000 of them) in the likeness of this gathering of princesses, of this series. See Lisa Orr, "Difference That Is Actually Sameness Mass-Reproduced: Barbie Joins the Princess Convergence," *Jeunesse: Young People, Texts, Cultures*, vol. 1, no. 1 (2009): 9.

7 DIM Girls

1 Kracauer, *The Mass Ornament*, 78.

2 Jean-Luc Nancy, *La communauté désoeuvrée* (Paris: Christian Bourgois, 1986) and *La communauté affrontée* (Paris: Minuit, 2001); Maurice Blanchot, *La communauté inavouable* (Paris: Minuit, 1983).

3 See Elisabeth Roudinesco's little essay *L'analyse, l'archive* (Paris: Bibliothèque nationale de France, 2001) and recent publications, in magazines or dailies, articles, reports, and documents, about the increase of cases of perverse narcissism in Western society.

4 Alain Badiou, "Intervention dans le cadre du Collège international de philosophie sur le livre de Giorgio Agamben: *la Communauté qui vient, théorie de la singularité quelconque*," transcription by François Duvert, www.entretemps.asso.fr.

5 Giorgio Agamben, *The Coming Community*, 18.

6 Ibid., 52, 55.

7 Ibid., 22.

8 Ibid., 59.

9 "Whatever singularity, which wants to appropriate belonging itself, its own being-in-language, and thus rejects all identity and every condition of belonging, is the principal enemy of the State. Wherever these singularities peacefully demonstrate their being in common there will be Tienanmen, and, sooner or later, the tanks will appear" (ibid., 86).

10 Ibid., 85.

11 Ibid., 47.

12 Ibid., 48.

13 Agamben, *What Is an Apparatus*, 24.

8 Tableaux Vivants

1 With the exception of the piece created for her wedding (*VBGBW*, 2000) and another in recent years, in a Catholic orphanage in the South Sudan, where she photographed herself as an haute-couture Madonna holding twin babies in her arms (*White Madonna with Twins*). The ensuing controversy, and Beecroft's expressed desire to adopt the children (which in the end did not happen), was documented in Pietra Brettkelly's film *The Art Star and the Sudanese Twins*, presented at the Sundance Film Festival in 2008. "The image of me with the twins wouldn't have been so powerful if I didn't wear the Margiela dress because then it also had a sinister edge; I am the greed, the perfection of the dress is the ephemeral fashion element, the correlative, the two kids represent vulnerability, needy, naked, and double so they can multiply as many times as you want." Cited by Miranda Purves, "Body of Work," *Elle*, May 1, 2008, www.elle.com. Following the presentation of Brettkelly's film, Beecroft became "unpopular, criticized for being a privileged white woman 'shopping for a baby,' and even received death threats. . . . 'Vanessa is one of those artists – and a lot of artists are like this – who can lose the ability to differentiate between her artistic fantasy and reality,' says [Jeffrey] Deitch [who discovered her twenty years ago]. 'It's part of what makes her great.'" In Amy Larocca, "For Kanye collaborator Vanessa Beecroft, people are the perfect palette," *New York Magazine*, August 9, 2016.

2 Purves, "Body of Work."

3 Judith Thurman, "The Wolf at the Door," *The New Yorker*, March 17, 2003, www.newyorker.com.

4 Christine Ross, *The Aesthetics of Disengagement: Contemporary Art and Depression* (Minneapolis: University of Minnesota Press, 2006), 61.

5 Beecroft describes her relationship to the performances: "What I like in the performance is the live event, the moment in which you don't really know what is happening. It is a way of formalizing an idea without conceptualizing it. I report the indefiniteness of the image that the girls create without having to theorize it. It is almost like a blurred picture, a painting by Richter. You don't see it clearly, and then it is gone." In Vanessa Beecroft, *Photographs, Films, Drawings* (Stuttgart: Hatje Cantz Publishers, 2004), 130.

6 Thurman, "The Wolf at the Door."

7 Slavoj Zizek, *Welcome to the Desert of the Real* (New York/London: Verso, 2002).

8 She conceptualizes the scene in terms of the exhibition space: for the Gagosian Gallery in London, the reference to Elizabeth I; for the Gunma Museum in Japan, members of the US Marines. . . .

9 Another controversial aspect of Beecroft's work: photos of this performance were sold for $40,000 to $80,000. The girls each earned $3,000 for being waxed, bleached, made up, and posing for three days – for as long as 15 hours during one of those days. See an

interview with the Guerilla Girls who infiltrated the performance: Kristen Raizada, "An Interview with the Guerilla Girls, Dyke Action Machine (DAM!), and the Toxic Titties," *NWSA Journal*, vol. 19, no. 1 (Spring 2007), https://muse.jhu.edu.

10 Beecroft's blind, problematic, and offensive relation to race has been criticized, most recently by Amy Larocca in her August 9, 2016, article "For Kanye collaborator Vanessa Beecroft, people are the perfect palette" (*New York Magazine*). Larocca reflects on the artist's complicated relationship to race: Beecroft operates so unusually with regard to race, with such entitled swagger, she seems to be living in something of a cave, entirely cut off from any public debate or conversation on topics of identity. She says race has always fascinated her, even during her childhood, when she rarely saw people of different races. In the course of this interview, Beecroft announces that she is working on a Barbie project for Mattel. "Perhaps," writes Larocca, quoting Beecroft, "some of them will have 'caramel Beyoncé skin,' acknowledging murmurings (including from her husband) that Beyoncé's 'Formation' video owes her some creative debt. But she doesn't get into it too deeply, she says, because she has only the vaguest idea that someone named 'Beyoncé' actually exists."

9 Like a Girl Takes Off Her Dress

1 A controversy that has only grown since the beginning of her collaboration with Kanye West, in regards to his fashion line *Yeezy Season 3*.

2 Ortega in Hanquez-Maincent, *Barbie, poupée totem*, 132.

3 Mannequin: from the Dutch *mannekijn*, "little man."

4 Jean-Luc Nancy, *La pensée dérobée* (Paris: Galilée, 2001), 35. In French, *dérober* means to steal or conceal, more than to remove a robe or dress, even though the verb is formed as *dé-rober*. – Trans.

5 Georges Didi-Huberman, *Ninfa moderna: Essai sur le drapé tombé* (Paris: Gallimard, 2002).

6 This term means at once a chrysalis, the labia minora, and a young goddess.

7 Didi-Huberman, *Ninfa moderna*, 36.

8 David Kishik, *The Power of Life: Agamben and the Coming Politics,* (Palo Alto, CA: Stanford Universty Press, 2012), 19.

9 Agamben, *What Is an Apparatus?*, 40.

10 Ibid., 53.

11 See the important testimonies of survivors of Nazi deportation (those of Elie Wiesel, Jorge Semprun, Charlotte Delbo, and Robert Antelme, among others, for the French domain) and the numerous studies about them.

12 "It is difficult to bear the sight of the thousands of naked corpses piled in common graves or carried on the shoulders of former camp guards, of those tortured bodies that even the SS could not name (we know from witnesses that under no circumstances were they to be called 'corpses' or 'cadavers,' but rather simply *Figuren*, figures, dolls)." Giorgio Agamben, *Remnants of Auschwitz: The Witness and the Archive*, trans. Daniel Heller-Roazen (New York: Zone Books, 1999), 50–51.

13 Agamben, *What Is an Apparatus*, 48. Fashion has a habit of reviving the past: some current trends were fashionable twenty or thirty years ago, and just when we thought they had disappeared forever, fashion revives them. The "hipster" phenomenon is a good example of fashion's anachronism (quotational, ironic).

14 Ibid.

15 "Thus we have passed from disguise-drapery/costume-drapery that makes us burst out laughing to shroud-drapery and, worst, to *the rag formed by the body itself* when sacrificed to the disfiguring violence of some myth, war, or rite." Didi-Huberman, *Ninfa moderna*, 109. In French, *drap* means bedsheet. – Trans.

16 Didi-Huberman, "To Render Sensible," in Alain Badiou et al., *What Is a People?*, trans. Jody Gladding (New York: Columbia University Press, 2016), 81.

10 Showgirls

1 *Girl Model*, directed by David Redmon and Ashley Sabin (Carnivalesque Films, 2012), 78 mins.

2 *Picture Me*, directed by Ole Schell and Sara Ziff (New York: 25th Frame & Digital Bazooka, 2010), 82 mins.

3 Ziff has also produced a film on the fashion industry and garment labourers. *Tangled Thread* (New York: stz films) tells the story of two labour activists, Ziff and Kalpona Akter, who try to unite fashion's most visible workers – fashion models – and least visible workers – women who work in garment factories in Bangladesh – in a fight for fair treatment and working conditions.

4 Angelica Pursley, "Money, celebrity, and race: The modeling industry laid bare," *CNN*, April 26, 2016. www.cnn.com.

5 "The Fashion Industry's Race Problem: Models of Color Rarely Get Hired," *Think-Progress*, August 9, 2013, http://thinkprogress.org. See also Hadley Freeman, "Why black models are rarely in fashion," *The Guardian*, February 18, 2014, www.theguardian.com.

6 Agamben, *Qu'est-ce que le contemporain?*, 31.

7 *Showgirls*, directed by Paul Verhoeven (Hollywood: United Artists, 1995), 128 mins.

8 Linda Williams, "Showgirls and Sex Acts," *Film Quarterly*, vol. 56, no. 3 (Spring 2003).

9 Olivia Rosenthal, *Ils ne sont pour rien dans mes larmes* (Paris: Verticales, 2012).

10 *Thelma and Louise*, directed by Ridley Scott (Hollywood: MGM, 1991), 130 mins.

11 Girl Tales

1 We must no doubt question recent versions of Snow White: *Mirror Mirror* (2012) and *Snow White and the Huntsman* (2012), in which the stepmother is wicked and Snow White invested with the power to eliminate. In *Mirror Mirror*, not only does the step-mother lose but youth wins out: "Age before beauty," says Snow White to the step-mother, now transformed. This rejection of the aging woman is not without political consequences. Giving girls back to girls must not occur at the expense of women no longer considered "young."

2 *Hard Candy*, directed by David Slade (Seattle, WA: Vulcan Productions, 2005), 104 mins; *The Brave One*, directed by Neil Jordan (Hollywood: Warner Bros., 2007), 122 mins.

3 Produced in 2005 and 2007 respectively, and these, along with other films such as *Death Sentence* (2008), signal a return of Hollywood to the vigilante movie, a come-back sometimes attributed to post–9/11 America.

4 Quoted in Andrew Lang, *The Blue Fairy Book* (London, ca. 1899), 51–53, www.pitt.edu.

5 Catherine Orenstein, *Little Red Riding Hood Uncloaked: Sex, Morality, and the Evolution of a Fairy Tale* (New York: Basic Books, 2003).

6 *Peau d'âne* is a well-known literary fairy tale published by Charles Perrault in 1695. – Trans.

7 "With its multiple interlockings, nesting dolls, there is no end to opening up this wolf, to seeing what is inside, for this ventriloquist is a champion ventripotent. . . . This tale is exhausting, it devours characters, it swallows as many as it produces." Anne-Marie Garat, *Une faim de loup: Lecture du Petit chaperon rouge* (Arles, France: Actes sud, 2005), 162 (our translation).

8 Garat compares the wolf's unreal act and the serial killer's: "The understatement dodges the cruelty, but not its imaginary reach. The scene unfolds at such speed that it becomes dreamlike, with the fantasy strangeness of visions. Thus, paradoxically,

connecting it with an abominable reality: serial killers and other crazed murderers, in the brutality and speed of execution of their actions, combine insanity and cold technical intelligence, savagery and maniacal precision" (ibid., 120).

9 In *Hard Candy*, it is not the hunter who pulls the little girl from the wolf's belly, but the girl who, figuratively, extracts the wolf from the hunter's body by removing his testicles.

10 Peter Sloterdijk, "The Time of the Crime of the Monstrous: On the Philosophical Justification of the Artificial," trans. Wieland Hoban, in Stuart Elden, ed., *Sloterdijk Now* (Cambridge: Polity, 2011), 165.

11 Ibid., 206.

12 *Alien: alienare*: to make strange, to make other; derived from *alienus*: other, itself derived from *alias* (alibi): elsewhere.

12 One for All, All for One

1 Bordeleau, *Foucault anonymat*, 81 (our translation).

2 Ibid., 82.

3 Ibid., 93.

4 Agamben, *What is an Apparatus?*, 14.

5 Ibid., 23.

6 *Barbara*, directed by Christian Petzold (Berlin: Schramm Film Koerner & Weber, 2012), 105 mins.

7 Ralf Schenk, "Life in a bubble," *Berliner Zeitung*, March 7, 2012, www.signandsight.com.

8 *A Woman In Berlin / Anonyma – Eine Frau in Berlin*, directed by Max Färberböck (Munich: Constantin Film, 2008), 131 mins.

9 Alan Gardiner, *Theory of Proper Names* (New York: Irvington, 1984).

10 Yaguello, *Les mots et les femmes*, 221–226 (our translation).

11 Ibid., 225.

12 Of course Yaguello is writing in 1978, and the question needs to be posed today. However, that is the period Petzold depicts in *Barbara*.

13 Ibid., 226.

14 Josée Yvon, *Danseuses-Mamelouk* (Montréal: VLB, 1982), 108 (our translation).

15 Josée Yvon (1950–1994). See her books *Filles-missiles* (Trois-Rivières, QC: Écrits des forges, 1986) and *Danseuses-Mamelouk*.

16 Éléonore Mercier, *Je suis complètement battue* (Paris: Minuit, 2010).

17 Lauren Strapagiel, "'One Photo a Day' Serbian Domestic Abuse Video Goes Viral," *Huffington Post*, March 20, 2013, www.huffingtonpost.ca.

13 Mirror, Mirror

1 John Berger, *Ways of Seeing* (London: Penguin, 1972), 47 (italics in original).

2 See her website, www.nellyarcan.com.

3 Nelly Arcan, *Burqa of Skin*, 36.

4 Emmanuel Levinas, *On Escape, De l'évasion*, trans. Bettina Bergo (Stanford, CA: Stanford University Press, 2003), 64.

5 Carol J. Adams, *The Pornography of Meat* (London: Bloomsbury Academic, 2004); Carol J. Adams and Josephine Donovan, eds., "Woman-Battering and Harm to Animals," in *Animals and Women: Feminist Theoretical Explorations* (Durham, NC: Duke University Press, 1999), 80.

6 "There would be no eating of domesticated animals if female animals weren't kept pregnant to produce the animals being consumed. There would be no milk, if cows weren't kept lactating; no eggs if chickens weren't kept ovulating. All flesh eaters

benefit from the alienated labor of the bitches, chicks, (mad) cows, and sows whose own bodies represent their labor and whose names reveal a double enslavement – the literal reproduction forced upon them, and the metaphoric enslavement that conveys female denigration, so that we human females become animals through insults, we become the bitches, chicks, cows, and sows, terms in which our bodies or movements are placed within an interpretative climate in which female freedom is not to be envisioned." Carol J. Adams, "An Animal Manifesto: Gender, Identity, and Vegan-Feminism in the Twenty-First Century," *Parallax*, no. 38 (2006): 120–128. See also the appendix to Lisa Kemmerer's book *Sister Species: Women, Animals, and Social Justice* (Chicago: University of Illinois Press, 2011).

7   Virginia Woolf, "The Plumage Bill," in *Animals and Women: Feminist Theoretical Explorations*, eds. Carol J. Adams and Josephine Donovan (Durham, NC: Duke University Press, 1995).

8   Carol J. Adams, *The Sexual Politics of Meat* (New York: Continuum, 1995), p. 80.

9   See Adams, *The Pornography of Meat*, for an impressive sampling of advertisements and publicity images representing women and meat as equivalents.

10   Davis, "From Hunting Grounds to Chicken Rights: My Story in an Eggshell," in Kemmerer, *Sister Species*, 128.

11   We could also add a reading of Marcela Iacub's novel *Beauty and Beast*, a narrative retelling of her romantic relationship with Dominique Strauss-Kahn that revisits Perrault's tale and, in a way, reverses the premise of Marie Darieussecq's *Truismes* (*Pig Tales: A Novel of Lust and Transformation*) (1996). In it, the man is a pig, but the man's porcine part is his best side.

12   Quoted in Charles Patterson, *Eternal Treblinka: Our Treatment of Animals and the Holocaust* (New York: Lantern Books, 2012), 165.

13   Theodor W. Adorno, *Minima Moralia*, trans. Dennis Redmond (1951 [2005]), www.marxists.org.

14   Quoted in Patterson, *Eternal Treblinka*, 165.

15   It should be noted that within the camps, the SS set up farms, slaughterhouses, and butchers' stalls to provide themselves with delicious meals, which they described in detail in their correspondence and diaries (recounted in Patterson, *Eternal Treblinka*).

16   Patterson, *Eternal Treblinka*, 28.

17   Quoted in ibid., 45.

18   Ibid., 47.

14   Bunnies

1   de Beauvoir, *The Second Sex*, 35–36.

2   Irene Lopez Rodriguez, "Of Women, Bitches, Chickens and Vixens: Animal Metaphors for Women and Animals in English and Spanish," *Culture, Language and Representation*, vol. 7 (2009): 77–100.

3   See the 1968 invitation, "No more Miss America!" reproduced here: www.feministzine.com.

4   Steven Watts, *Mr. Playboy: Hugh Hefner and the American Dream* (New Jersey: John Wiley & Sons, 2008), 232.

5   In an article published in *Ms Magazine* on September 20, 2011, Gail Dines asks what is most offensive about NBC's pilot episode of the series *The Playboy's Club*, as it reproduces the sexual and racial dynamics of the original Playboy economy: "What is the 'bunnies' spontaneously breaking into song, or the house mother earnestly lecturing the women to be the 'very best bunny they can be,' or maybe the moment when the only black bunny (indeed the only black person in the whole show) tells

her bunny comrades that her life's dream is to be the first-ever 'chocolate' Playboy centerfold?" (Gail Dines, "Yes, The Playboy Club IS That Bad," *Ms Magazine*, September 20, 2011, http://msmagazine.com). When the pilot was aired, Gloria Steinem herself encouraged viewers to boycott it.

6 Watts, *Mr. Playboy*, 234.

7 Ibid.

8 Ibid., 235.

9 Ibid., 240.

10 Ibid., 39. Also, these words from ex-Bunny Izabella St. James: "Bunnies are not born; bunnies are made. And they are made with the help of a whole army of people." *Bunny's Tales: Behind Closed Doors at the Playboy Mansion* (Philadelphia: Running Press, 2009), 193.

11 Gloria Steinem, "I Was a Playboy Bunny" (1963), in *Outrageous Acts and Everyday Rebellions* (New York: Holt, Rinehart and Winston, 1995), 44.

12 Ibid., 57.

13 Gloria Steinem, "What Playboy Doesn't Know About Could Fill a Book," *McCall's*, October 1970.

14 Ibid., 75.

15 Ibid., 66.

16 Beatriz Preciado, *Pornotopia, an essay on Playboy's architecture & biopolitics* (New York: Zone Books/MIT Press, 2014), 42.

17 In 2001, at 75 years old, Hefner, interviewed in *Vanity Fair*, said: "There is something cute and sweet about the way they all have this kind of blond-girl-next-door look. . . . We do all kinds of wonderful things together. We go to Disneyland together. We go out to the movies, and we go out to the clubs." Quoted in Joanna Pitman, *On Blondes* (Stirlingshire, UK: Palimpsest Book, 2003), 252.

18 Preciado, *Pornotopia*, 31.

19 Ibid., 37.

20 Ibid., 33.

21 Ibid., 34.

22 Quoted in Carrie Pitzulo, *Bachelors and Bunnies: The Sexual Politics of Playboy* (Chicago: University of Chicago Press, 2011), 27.

23 "It is really the male play of turning the page that operates the transformation of the next-door neighbor into a real Playmate, that converts dressed into undressed, folded into opened, hidden into exposed, private into public, and finally the 'peeping' into 'instant sex.' The unfolding of the four-page centerfold assured the reversibility effect. . . . The simple operation of turning the page established a new relationship between the eye and the hand (both reading and masturbating organs) and produced the Playmate and pleasure (immaterial products) as the result of the very exercise of reading" (ibid., 57–58).

24 Nathalie Collard, "*Sex and the City*, déjà 15 ans," *La Presse*, June 17, 2013, www.lapresse.ca (our translation).

25 Virginie Despentes, *King Kong Theory*, trans. Stéphanie Benson (London: Serpent's Tail, 2009), 88–89.

26 Ibid., 79.

27 Created by Ilene Chaiken and presented by Showtime from 2004 to 2009.

28 *Chéries Chéris*, "Virginie Despentes raconte Mutantes!" (blog), November 13, 2010, http://cheriescheris.blogspot.ca.

29 A category in which I would include the queen of porn studies, Linda Williams, as well as actresses and directors Ovidie, Émilie Jouvet, Wendy Delorme, Sasha Gray, Maria Llopis . . . liberated hard-core porn workers who attract all eyes and provoke a

distressed feeling, be it of desire or of rejection. See Despentes, *King Kong Theory*, 81.
30 Ibid., 178.

15 Blonds

1 Pitman, *On Blondes*, 187.
2 See Hélène Frappat, "L'invention de la blondeur," *Les Inrockuptibles*, special issue, "Marilyn: Au-delà de l'icône" (2012), 30–31 (our translation).
3 Ibid., 31.
4 See the issue of *Les Inrockuptibles* for a sampling of "covers"/remakes, pastiches, and references, and also the special issue of *Télérama*, "Marilyn," both published on the occasion of the fiftieth anniversary of her death in 1962.
5 Thank you to Rania Aoun, a student at l'Université du Québec à Montréal, for her research that identified echoes between portraits of Nelly Arcan and of Marilyn Monroe, and revealed, in Nelly Arcan's photos, a reproduction, a pastiche of camera angles and editing choices used for Marilyn Monroe.
6 Nelly Arcan, review of Michel Schneider's book *Marilyn's Last Sessions*, trans. Will Hobson (Edinburgh: Canongate Books, 2011), http://fr.canoe.ca.
7 Ibid.
8 Schneider, *Marilyn's Last Sessions*, 288.
9 Ibid., 162.
10 Tony Curtis, *The Making of Some Like It Hot: My Memories of Marilyn Monroe and the Classic American Movie* (Hoboken, NJ: Wiley, 2009), 79.
11 Ibid., 1.
12 Schneider, *Marilyn's Last Sessions*.
13 Ibid., 65.
14 Nelly Arcan, *Hysteric*, trans. David Homel and Jacob Homel (Vancouver: Anvil Press, 2014).
15 Ibid.
16 Normand de Bellefeuille, "Introduction," in Huguette Gaulin, *Lecture en vélocipède* (Montreal, Les Herbes rouges, 2007), 8. Huguette Gaulin is a Quebec writer who committed suicide publicly by self-immolation in Montreal's Old Port in 1972, while screaming, "You have destroyed the beauty of the world!" – Trans.
17 Italics in original. – Trans.
18 Italics in original. – Trans.
19 Arcan, *Hysteric*.
20 Ibid., 49.
21 Ibid., 77.
22 Ibid., 43.
23 Georges Didi-Huberman, *Survivance des lucioles* (Paris: Minuit, 2009).
24 Arcan, *Hysteric*, 135.
25 Ibid., 80.
26 Didi-Huberman, *Survivance des lucioles*, 10–11 (our translation).
27 In Schneider, *Marilyn's Last Sessions*, 268.
28 Didi-Huberman, *Survivance des lucioles*, 11 (our translation).
29 Ibid., 19.
30 Ibid., 49.
31 Schneider, *Marilyn's Last Sessions*, 227–228.
32 Ibid., 229.
33 Ibid., 290.
34 Ibid., 250.
35 Ibid., 262.

36 Ibid., 10.
37 Ibid.
38 Ibid., 393.
39 Ibid., 219.

16 *Girls* 1

1 "Hitchcock didn't just take away. He ground down his blondes and destroyed them. . . . The blonde – whether buxom, coolly elegant or bland – was still the dominant female type in Hollywood and as such covered the aspirational ground for much of America." Joanna Pitman, *On Blondes*, 232, 233.

2 As Caitlin Flanagan suggests in "Inventing Marilyn," *The Atlantic*, March 2013, 92–102.

3 See Mike Trapp, "If People Talked About *Seinfeld* Like They Talk About *Girls*," *College Humor*, March 4, 2013, www.collegehumor.com. In this parodic article the writer subjects *Seinfeld* to the same criticism levelled at *Girls*.

4 Dunham has been widely criticized – including for representing only educated, middle-class young whites, for showing stereotypical sex roles and relationships, and for being politically incorrect. I'm disinclined to bring *Girls* to trial here. However, one must acknowledge the limitations that come along with choosing four white, middle-class young women as heroines. As Roxane Gay writes in *Bad Feminist*: "The networks offer a numbing sea of whiteness save for the shows produced by Shonda Rhimes (*Grey's Anatomy, Private Practice, Scandal*), who makes a deliberate effort to address race, gender, and, to a lesser extent, sexuality when she casts. Beyond that, black people – all people of color, really – only get to see themselves as lawyers and sassy friends and, of course, as The Help. Even when a show promises to break new ground, like Lena Dunham's *Girls* . . . we are forced to swallow more of the same – a general erasure or ignorance of race." (New York: Harper, 2014, 5.)

5 At times, the world of *Girls* recalls that of American photographer Nan Goldin. *Girls*, "The Return," episode 1.6, directed by Lena Dunham, written by Lena Dunham and Judd Apatow (HBO, May 20, 2012).

6 Rebecca Mead, "Downtown's daughter: Lena Dunham cheerfully exposes her privileged life," *The New Yorker*, November 15, 2010, www.newyorker.com.

7 "A Conversation with Lena Dunham and Judd Apatow," *Girls: The Complete First Season*, DVD (New York: HBO Home Video, 2012).

8 *Girls*, "Vagina Panic," episode 1.2, directed by Lena Dunham, written by Lena Dunham (HBO, April 22, 2012).

9 Rochelle Keyhan, "Girls vs Sex and the City: Can You Even Compare?", *HBO Watch*, February 8, 2014, http://hbowatch.com; Britt Aboutaleb, "All the Ways in Which 'Girls' Has Already Been Compared to SATC," *Elle*, April 13, 2012, www.elle.com.

10 I.e., Jean de la Fontaine and his classic *Fables*, 1621–1695. – Trans.

11 Agamben, *The Coming Community*, 2 (italics in original).

12 Elaine Blair, "The Loves of Lena Dunham," *The New York Review of Books*, June 7, 2012, www.nybooks.com.

13 *Girls*, "Vagina Panic."

14 In fact there is a similar scene in the second season. This time it does not feature Hannah but rather Adam's new girlfriend (a relationship claiming to be "normal"). Moreover, at the end of the scene, the camera clearly shows the sperm covering the young woman's chest – a "money shot" typical of porn, but as yet unseen on television.

15 Blair, "The Loves of Lena Dunham."

16 Linda Williams, *Hard Core: Power, Pleasure, and the "Frenzy of the Visible,"* Expanded Edition (Berkeley: University of California Press, 1999).

17 *Girls*, "Pilot," episode 1.1, directed by Lena Dunham, written by Lena Dunham (HBO, April 15, 2012).

18 Blair, "The Loves of Lena Dunham."

17 Girls 2

1 This is the cause of their initial encounter: Hannah admits to Joshua that she dumps the coffee grounds from her workplace into his private trashcan, in front of his house, to get a sense of how it feels to own your own trashcan.

2 *Girls*, "Pilot."

3 *Girls*, "I Get Ideas," episode 2.2, directed by Lena Dunham, written by Jenni Konner and Lena Dunham (HBO, January 20, 2013).

4 *Girls*, "Together," episode 2.10, directed by Lena Dunham, written by Judd Apatow and Lena Dunham (HBO, March 17, 2013).

5 Carrie's relationship with the wealthy Big (clearly developed in both feature films based on the series) is but one example.

6 *Girls*, "One Man's Trash," episode 2.5, directed by Richard Shepard, written by Lena Dunham (HBO, February 10, 2013).

7 *Bartleby, the Scrivener: A Story of Wall Street*, 1853. – Trans.

8 Gilles Deluze, *Essays Critical and Clinical*, trans. Daniel W. Smith and Michael A. Greco (New York: Verso, 1998), 69.

9 Slavoj Zizek, *The Parallax View* (Cambridge/London: The MIT Press, 2006), 382.

10 Diana Fuss, *Essentially Speaking: Feminism, Nature and Difference* (New York: Routledge, 1989).

11 A study should be done of Dunham's humour, her particular use of language – through paratax, unusual word combinations, and twists of meaning, all accomplished outside slapstick's habitual economy, to the benefit of language rendered slightly unrecognizable, surprising: "Good day, ladies – I mean, whores"; "I can't work for free anymore. . . ."

18 Street Girls

1 Women's sports teams are an interesting case of serial girls, as can be seen in films dealing with female friendship, competition sports, and female desire (such as Céline Sciamma's feature film *Water Lilies* [2007], which takes place in the swimming world).

2 *Envoyé special*, "Femmes: le harcèlement de rue," Virginie Vilar, France2, March 12, 2013.

3 Marie Cardinal, *In Other Words*, trans. Amy Cooper (Bloomington & Indianapolis: Indiana University Press, 1995), 109.

4 Virginies Despentes, *Rape Me*, trans. Bruce Benderson (New York: Grove Press, 2002).

5 *Courrier International*, "Les insoumises," no. 1161 (January 31–February 6, 2013).

6 I'm talking about women, but of course I don't mean to exclude other populations in precarious situations, those discarded lives whose basic needs, such as health and security, are constantly ignored.

7 Since, as we know, genders do not exist in a vacuum. It is rare to find human specimens in whom chromosomes, biochemistry, genital organs, genetic code, all coincide to result in . . . a *perfect* woman or man. On this subject see, among others, Kate Bornstein, Judith Butler, Judith Halberstam, Luce Irigaray, Hélène Cixous, and Monique Wittig.

8 Judith Butler, "'We the People': Thoughts on Freedom of Assembly," trans. Jody Gladding, in *What Is a People*, eds. Alain Badiou et al. (New York: Columbia University Press, 2016), 51.

9 Ibid., 58–59.

10 Ibid., 59.

11 Ibid., 60.

12 Ibid., 63.

13 At the time of writing (September 4, 2013), a growing buzz surrounds Kitty Green's documentary *Ukraine Is Not a Brothel*, presented at the Venice Mostra. Indeed, rumour has it that it was a man, Viktor Svyatski, who founded the Femen movement and chose its members, keeping them firmly under his hold until they broke free. So far, few dailies have relayed this information (except the *Sunday Times* and the *Independent*, both UK papers). It is therefore difficult to sort out what is misinformation (a process Femen has well been the object of) and what is the truth. Given that the documentary is unavailable at the time of writing, I'll adhere to Inna Schevchenko's words in *The Guardian*, September 5, 2013, www.theguardian.com, where she confirms Svyatski's presence and his hold (his control, his rage), but denies the fact that he founded the movement (which was born, instead, from a women's collective). She also specifies that Femen settled in France partly to get rid of Svyatski, and partly to allow the movement to grow into what it is today. In addition, notes Shevchenko, there is a connection between Femen members' struggle against male domination over their private lives (embodied by Svyatski) and the struggle they are leading against this domination worldwide. In every case, the movement, in all its complexity, represents a feminist phenomenon worthy of analysis.

14 *Technikart* 167 (November 2012).

15 Gillian Schutte, "Beware the Naked Women!" *The South African Civil Society Information Service*, June 7, 2012, http://sacsis.org.za.

16 Alice Schwarzer, in Dialika Neufield (2012), "The Body Politic: Getting Naked to Change the World," Spiegel Online International, trans. Christopher Sultan, www.spiegel.de.

17 Which reminds me of a strategy outlined in the film *The Life of David Gale*, in which an activist against the death penalty stages a crime (of which he is later falsely accused) in order to prove that not only does American justice send innocents to the gallows, but also that the death penalty is an inhumane practice.

18 As I finish writing this book, some group members were badly beaten, and Femen headquarters in Paris, at the Lavoir Moderne, were destroyed by fire.

19 Judith Butler, " 'We the People,' " 64.

20 Michel de Certeau, *The Practice of Everyday Life*, trans. Steven F. Rendall (Berkeley: University of California Press, 2011).

21 Jewish French philosopher Emmanuel Levinas (1906–1995). In *Ethics and Infinity* (Pittsburgh: Duquesne University Press, 1985), he writes: "The first word of the face is the 'Thou shalt not kill.' It is an order. There is a commandment in the appearance of the face, as if a master spoke to me. However, at the same time, the face of the Other is destitute; it is the poor for whom I can do all and to whom I owe all" (89).

22 Carol Cadwalladr, "Pussy Riot: Will Vladimir Putin Regret Taking On Russia's Cool Women Punks?" *The Guardian*, July 29, 2012, www.theguardian.com.

23 *Pussy Riot: A Punk Prayer*, a documentary broadcast on HBO in June 2013, highlights the connection between the state and the Orthodox Church in today's Russia.

24 *60 Minutes*, "Pussy Riot punk band remains defiant of Putin's Russia," CBS News, June 23, 2013.

25 And even today in 2013, while still imprisoned (the Russian government is denying them early release), they continue to write. See Nadezhda Tolokonnikova's open letter "Pussy Riot Denied Parole: Why I Am Going on Hunger Strike," *n+ one Magazine*, September 23, 2013, https://nplusonemag.com.

26 Interviewed during her visit to the United States, one group member noted that while Pussy Riot are grateful for the support of Western artists such as Madonna, they are wary of becoming a brand: "We are against corporations using us as a brand or trademark. We're not selling anything." When someone suggested that perhaps they are sell-

ing freedom, they countered: "You cannot buy freedom. It's not for sale." In Joshua Keating, "Breakfast with Pussy Riot," *Foreign Policy*, June 7, 2013, https://foreignpolicy.com.

27 Slavoj Zizek, "The True Blasphemy," *Dangerous Minds*, August 10, 2012, http://dangerousminds.net.

28 One of the two sentenced Pussy Riot members, Nadezhda Tolokonnikova, claims in an interview that she's asexual, that she uses her body like painters use colours. *Pussy Riot: A Punk Prayer*, directed by Mike Lerner and Maxim Pozdorovkin (London: Roast Beef Productions, 2013), 88 mins.

29 *60 Minutes*, "Pussy Riot punk band."

30 Ibid.

31 I'm referring to the title of his play with feminist overtones, *Who's Afraid of Virginia Woolf?* (1962).

32 *60 Minutes Overtime*, "Why the Pussy Riot Story Is Important," June 23, 2013, www.cbsnews.com.

Conclusion: Firefly Girls

1 Suzanne Moore, "Pussy Riot are a reminder that revolution always begins in culture," *The Guardian*, August 1, 2012, www.theguardian.com.

2 Didi-Huberman, *Survivance des lucioles*, 51 (our translation) (italics in original).

3 Ibid., 74.

4 Ibid., 101.

5 Ibid.

6 Ibid., 132–133.

7 Ibid., 17.

8 Charlotte Beradt, *The Third Reich of Dreams* (New York: Quadrangle Books, 1968).

9 Agamben, *The Coming Community*, 24.

10 Ibid.

Shelfie

An **ebook** edition is available for $2.99
with the purchase of this print book.

CLEARLY PRINT YOUR NAME ABOVE IN UPPER CASE

Instructions to claim your eBook edition:
1. Download the Shelfie app for Android or iOS
2. Write your name in **UPPER CASE** above
3. Use the Shelfie app to submit a photo
4. Download your eBook to any device

ISBN 978-1-77113-185-8